The truth ab

Or, Through the Emeralc

Alexander Corkey

(Contributor: William Jennings Bryan)

Alpha Editions

This edition published in 2024

ISBN : 9789362517920

Design and Setting By
Alpha Editions
www.alphaedis.com
Email - info@alphaedis.com

As per information held with us this book is in Public Domain.
This book is a reproduction of an important historical work. Alpha Editions uses the best technology to reproduce historical work in the same manner it was first published to preserve its original nature. Any marks or number seen are left intentionally to preserve its true form.

Contents

PREFACE ....- 1 -
INTRODUCTORY CHAPTER ....- 2 -
CHAPTER I ....- 5 -
CHAPTER II ....- 10 -
CHAPTER III ....- 15 -
CHAPTER IV ....- 19 -
CHAPTER V ....- 23 -
CHAPTER VI ....- 25 -
CHAPTER VII ....- 29 -
CHAPTER VIII ....- 32 -
CHAPTER IX ....- 37 -
CHAPTER X ....- 41 -
CHAPTER XI ....- 46 -
CHAPTER XII ....- 51 -
CHAPTER XIII ....- 55 -
CHAPTER XIV ....- 59 -
CHAPTER XV ....- 63 -
CHAPTER XVI ....- 67 -
CHAPTER XVII ....- 71 -
CHAPTER XVIII ....- 76 -
CHAPTER XIX ....- 79 -

PREFACE

THE aeroplane is man's latest invention. Through it man has become lord of the air. The steamship and steam engine had already given him victory over sea and land. Now he is complete master of the situation.

One of the most delightful uses of the aeroplane is in sightseeing. Aerial tourist travel will soon become popular, as a bird's-eye view of a country is the most satisfactory of all.

For several reasons, however, many will be unable to enjoy this latest luxury, traveling IN THE BODY, but WITH THE MIND everyone who desires can enjoy in the following pages, an aeroplane trip through Ireland, fairest of all lands.

This mental excursion in the aeroplane has obvious advantages over a like physical experience, as every aeronaut will cheerfully acknowledge. Future aerial travelers over Erin will be able to witness to the truthfulness of this bird's-eye view of Ireland, and I trust the historical allusions will add to the interest of our survey of the island's lovely scenes. The visits to Irish homes, and the glimpses of Irish character will also, I am sure, be enjoyed.

I wish to thank Hon. William Jennings Bryan for the Introductory Chapter, in which, from the viewpoint of a practical statesman, he shows the bright future of the Emerald Isle. The full account of this famous visit of his to Ireland was published in the Commoner, which owns the copyright.

THE AUTHOR.

INTRODUCTORY CHAPTER

SHOWING THE BRIGHT FUTURE OF IRELAND

BY

HON. WILLIAM JENNINGS BRYAN

MY visit to Ireland was too brief to enable me to look into the condition of the tenants in the various parts of the island, but by the courtesy of the Lord Mayor of Dublin, Mr. Timothy Harrington, and Mr. John Dillon, both members of Parliament, I met a number of the prominent representatives of Ireland in national politics.

It is true that home rule has not yet been secured, but the contest for home rule has focused attention upon the industrial and political condition of Erin, and a number of remedial measures have been adopted.

First, the tenant was given title to his improvements and then the amount of the rent was judicially determined. More recently the authorities have been building cottages for the rural laborers. Over 15,000 of these cottages have already been erected and arrangements are being made for some 19,000 more. These are much more comfortable than the former dwellings, and much safer from a sanitary point of view. The recent Land Purchase Act, which went into effect on November first, (1903), seems likely to exert a very great influence upon the condition of the people. According to its terms the Government is to buy the land from the landlord and sell it to the tenants.

As the Government can borrow money at a lower rate than the ordinary borrower, it is able to give the tenant much better terms than he gets from his present landlord, and at the same time purchase the land of the landlord at a price that is equitable. The landlords are showing a disposition to comply with the spirit of the law, although some of them are attempting to get a larger price for their land than it was worth prior to the passage of the law.

The purpose of the law is to remove from politics the landlord question, which has been a delicate one to deal with. Most of the larger estates were given to the ancestors of the present holders, and many of the owners live in England and collect their rents through a local agent. The new law makes the Government the landlord; and the tenant, by paying a certain annual sum for 63 years, becomes the owner of the fee. He has the privilege of paying all, or any part, at any time, and can dispose of his interest.

The settlement which is now being effected not only removes the friction which has existed between the tenant and the landlord, but puts the tenant in a position where he can appeal to the Government with reasonable certainty of redress in case unforeseen circumstances make his lot harder than at present anticipated.

The assurance that he will become the owner of the fee will give to the Irish farmer an ambition that has heretofore been wanting, for he will be able to save without fear of an increase in the rent.

Not only is the land question in process of settlement, but there has been at the same time other improvements which make for the permanent progress of the people. There is a constant increase in educational facilities, and a large number of co-operative banks have been established. Agricultural societies have been formed for the improvement of crops and stock, and the trend is distinctly upward. The Irish leaders have not obtained all that they labored for—there is much to be secured before their work is complete, but when the history of Ireland is written, the leaders now living will be able to regard with justifiable pride the results of their devotion and sacrifice and their names will be added to the long list of Irish patriots and statesmen.

In Dublin I paid my respects to Lord Dudley, Lieutenant Governor of Ireland, whose residence, the Viceregal Lodge, is in Phoenix Park, and found him so genial and affable a host that I am led to hope that in his administration of the executive branch of the Government he will make the same attempt at just treatment that parliament has made in the enactment of the recent land measures.

Dublin is a very substantial looking city and much more ancient in appearance than Belfast, the latter reminding one more of an enterprising American city. We did not have a chance to visit any of the industries of Dublin, and only a linen factory and a shipyard in Belfast, but as the linen factory, The York Street Linen Mills, was one of the largest in Ireland, and the shipyard, Harland and Wolff's, the largest in the world, they gave some idea of the industrial possibilities of the island.

Queenstown, Ireland, the first town to greet the tourist when he reaches Northern Europe and the last to bid him farewell when he departs, is a quaint and interesting old place. Here the returning traveller has a chance to spend any change which he has left, for blackthorn canes and shillelaghs, "Robert Emmett" and "Harp of Erin" handkerchiefs and lace collars are offered in abundance. At Queenstown one can hear the Irish brogue in all its richness and, if he takes a little jaunt about the town, he can enjoy the humor for which the Irish are famed.

To one accustomed to the farms of the Mississippi and the Missouri valleys, the little farms of Ireland seem contracted indeed, but what they lack in size they make up in thoroughness of cultivation. The farm houses are not large, but from the railroad train they looked neat and well kept.

There is a general desire among the leaders of thought in Ireland to check the emigration from that country. They feel that Ireland, under fair conditions, can support a much larger population than she now has. Ireland, they say, has been drained of many of its most enterprising and vigorous sons and daughters. It is hardly probable that the steps already taken will entirely check the movement towards the United States, but there is no doubt that the inhabitants of Ireland and their friends across the water contemplate the future *With Brighter Hopes and Anticipations* than they have for a century.

CHAPTER I

BEGINNING OF MY AEROPLANE TRIP THROUGH IRELAND

IT all happened in this way. Early last summer I was travelling through Ohio and came to the prosperous city of Dayton. While spending a few days visiting in this enterprising city, a friend met me, and proposed to call on the Wright Brothers, who had won wide fame as the men who knew how to fly.

I was rather skeptical about a man contesting the atmosphere with the fowls of the air. I had a private opinion that Mother Earth was meant for man, and that the nearer he kept to it the better. I went to see these aeronauts with a prejudice against the flying business.

We soon found the airship factory, and we were introduced to Mr. Wilbur Wright. He greeted us very cordially, and even took us around his factory, showing us an aeroplane and explaining its workings. I was astonished at the simplicity of the airship and was impressed with the enthusiasm of the successful young aeronaut. I began to thaw out. I asked a lot of questions. Before half an hour had passed by I was a convert to the flying business, and made up my mind that Mr. Wright was a "bird." He had discovered not only how to fly, but also, which is more important, how to light.

That was the beginning of my interest in aeroplanes. I do not expect that anything wonderful would have come out of my Dayton experience had I not journeyed the next week to New York State to visit an old-time friend, Mr. Mike Connor. Naturally, I began to display my new-found knowledge about aeronautics on the first opportunity. To my great surprise I found that Mr. Connor was also an enthusiastic aeroplanist. I found he knew all about flying. When I expressed wonder at his knowledge of this recent art of cleaving the heaven's blue, he told me he had been studying the matter for a long time. He said he could get few of his friends to take any stock in this latest victory of man over nature, and he was delighted to find me a sympathetic listener to his descriptions of the coming uses of flying machines.

Looking carefully around the room, as if to see that no unfriendly ear could hear, he finally confessed to me in a stage whisper:

"I have an aeroplane of my own. I bought it two months ago, and I can now fly with it beautifully."

"Good," I cried, "let me see it."

He at once took me out to the shed where he kept the "bird." I looked it over with intense interest, which pleased my good friend, Mike, (as I must call him) very much. It was a Wright aeroplane, about the same size as the one Mr. Wilbur Wright had shown me at Dayton. The two main planes, like the top and bottom of a street car, were 40 feet long and 7 feet wide. The distance between the upper and lower planes was 6 feet. These planes were covered with a stout cloth, like tent cloth. There were two small horizontal planes in front, controlled by levers, by which the aeroplane was raised or lowered at will when it was in the air. At the rear there was also a double set of planes, vertically placed, to assist in turning the airship, just as a helm turns a ship in the water. Motion was generated by two large propellers, seven feet long, made of spruce wood, which ran in opposite directions. Power was furnished by a compact, 25-horse power motor, which Mike, whom I knew to be an expert with gasoline engines, said was one of the best he ever handled.

"Just as reliable as steam," he assured me, when I spoke of the unreliability of the ordinary motor.

Mike explained to me how to start, how to rise and descend, and how to turn in the air.

I asked him why he had not let me know about this new treasure before, and he told me his friends to whom he had spoken about it had treated him so coldly, that he had ceased to mention the matter, but he had quietly been practicing with his machine until now he was able to fly anywhere. There was a large meadow back of his house, surrounded by thick groves, and in this secluded spot he had spent weeks perfecting himself in the art of flying.

As it was too late that day for a flight he promised to take me on my first jaunt among the clouds next morning.

I had known Mike Connor since he was a boy. His father had left him a lot of money, but he was not the usual wild kind of heir. He looked after his estate closely, but, having a heap of time on his hands, he was always ready for a diversion. When the bicycles first came out, he had two or three of the finest makes. He was the very first in his neighborhood to purchase an automobile, and he soon became an expert with his motor car. Accordingly, I was not surprised to know that he had so soon mastered the use of the aeroplane.

When we came back to the house he asked me suddenly:

"Jack, what are you going to do this summer?"

"I have been planning," I replied, "to take a run across the fish pond and visit old Ireland again."

"Good," he fairly shouted.

I looked at him a little curiously, wondering why he was so interested in my visit to the Emerald Isle.

"Let us go together," he continued enthusiastically, "and take the aeroplane."

This was certainly a novel proposition, and I laughed so heartily at the idea of flying through Ireland that Mike got impatient.

"Don't you think we can do it?" he asked.

"Let us wait till morning," I answered evasively, "and we will see about it." Mike's face fell, and I could see he thought I was not a thorough convert to the aeroplane art.

There is something of the Scotchman about me, and I wanted to know a little more about the "bird" business before I started on a vacation trip with wings. An Irish bog would not be a bad place for an aeronaut to alight in case he had to descend unceremoniously, but I didn't want to spoil a nice outing in Ireland by breaking my neck trying to fly.

The next morning we were up with the birds and soon had the aeroplane all ready for a flight. The Wright aeroplane ascends from a "starting rail," which is merely a stout board turned up on end.

The meadow was an ideal place to fly. It was an immense level field, about half a mile long, and quarter of a mile broad. I had all confidence in Mike and had no reason to believe he meant to destroy me, but I was just a little shaky as I climbed up into the second seat over the motor.

Mike vaulted easily into his seat, started the motor, and in a few seconds we were off. I can never describe the excitement of the next ten minutes. We rose to the height of about 80 feet, and then sailed rapidly round and round the field. The sensation of flying was something entirely new. I was exhilarated, charmed, delighted. After I became a little used to it I was able to observe the field below, which glided under us with marvelous speed.

After ten minutes of this thrilling experience Mike decided to land, as he did not wish to try my nerves too severely the first time. The landing was perfect. Mike shut off the motor at a height of 70 feet, and the aeroplane came gliding down like a big bird. I could not tell just when we came to earth, so gently did the airship alight. It glided along on its runners for a short distance and then came quietly to a stop.

I stepped out on the grass like a man in a dream.

"How did you like it?" asked Mike.

For answer I fairly hugged him. He was pleased and asked at once about a trip through Ireland.

"It would be grand," I exclaimed, "let us go."

We had several other flights together and we were both confident that we could have a glorious time in the Emerald Isle with an airship.

We soon completed our arrangements. The aeroplane was taken to pieces and carefully packed. Each box was marked "Queenstown."

In three weeks' time we were ready to start. We booked on the Lusitania, and, as the boxes, in which our aeroplane was stored, were taken on board as baggage, we landed in five days at Queenstown, airship and all.

I had crossed the Atlantic several times before, but this voyage was the most exciting of all. We sat on deck and talked of our plans when we landed. Mike was sure of his ability to fly a day at a time, and so we outlined a strenuous program. I was well acquainted with Ireland, and I had marked our stopping places as we would fly through the island.

Sometimes fear of failure would take possession of my mind. The whole thing was so novel. Such a thing as flying round a country on a sightseeing trip had never been attempted. I was fearful I had been rash.

A talk with Mike always sent these fears to the winds. He had no fears whatever.

As Mike was to have the chief share in piloting our airship, I decided to take generous notes and prepare a full account of the places we visited and our most exciting experiences as we flew over the green fields of Erin. From these notes I have prepared for the world the account of our trip which is found in the following chapters.

We had not breathed a word about our plans to anyone on board during our voyage across the Atlantic, and when we landed at Queenstown we quietly sent on our "baggage" to Cork, and followed ourselves that evening. We had planned to begin our flight from Cork. We expected to fly around the island in a couple of days and then visit some attractive places one by one. We were compelled to change this plan, as we shall see.

After a good night's rest at the Imperial Hotel in Cork, we "assembled," as aeronauts say, the various parts of our airship the next morning on a level field just outside the city.

We avoided the public as much as possible, and the few people who came around found us non-committal, and wondered what we were doing.

THROUGH THE EMERALD ISLE WITH AN AEROPLANE.

THROUGH THE EMERALD ISLE WITH AN AEROPLANE.

In the evening when we were left alone, about nine o'clock, (it is still quite light at this time in Ireland during July) we made a short trial ascent. Our first flight beneath the kindly Irish skies was a complete success. Everything was working beautifully.

Well satisfied with our first day's work we returned to our hotel for the night. Our plan was to fly the first day as far as the Giant's Causeway, going up the West side of the island. On the second day we expected to return to Cork and make trips here and there after that.

We had another good night's rest, and rose with the sun, or rather a little before it. We found our aeroplane in the field as we left it, and after carefully examining every part, Mike said:

"All right, Jack. Let us start."

I climbed up on my seat. Mike started the motor. The machine began to move along the starting rail, and rose like a bird. When we had gone up to about the height of 200 feet we circled around over Cork. In the dawning light we could see the strange tower of the Church of Saint Mary Shandon, St. Patrick's Street, and the beautiful Cathedral of St. Finbar's. I could also distinguish Queen's College.

Turning in a northwestern direction, Mike said to me:

"Now we're off."

We were speeding through the air towards Killarney.

CHAPTER II

FLYING OVER KILLARNEY IN AN AIRSHIP

IT was just 4:30 by my watch as we started from Cork on that eventful 11th day of July. There was good daylight, but the city was still wrapped in its slumbers.

It was a beautiful summer morning and our spirits rose with the aeroplane. We began the strangest trip through Ireland that was ever made by man. I can never forget the sight of the green fields of County Cork that morning. It was a scene of peaceful loveliness.

The first place of interest we passed over was Blarney Castle, which is only five miles from Cork. We swept directly over the famous ruin, and I had a strange feeling as I looked down on the far-famed fortress from my aerial seat. As I had been at Blarney Castle before I was able to locate that part of the wall where the Blarney Stone is seen. I tried to point it out to Mike, but, before I could get the place described, we had flown over it. We learned that to describe anything like that on the aeroplane you have to look as far ahead as possible. I had no idea the country around Blarney was so beautiful until I had a good bird's eve view of it. I was convinced that we would see all the scenic beauties of Ireland from our aeroplane as they had never been seen before.

The distance from Cork to Killarney is 50 miles as the crow flies, and as we were now traveling like crows we measured distances as they did. We could see the River Lee at our left as it meandered through the neat farms and little fields of the Cork farmers. The pleasant-looking cottages fairly flew beneath us. We were surprised to see so much of County Cork under cultivation, as we expected to see it all in grazing land. I found out later that under the beneficent new Land Laws most of these small farmers now own their own farms, and that this part of Ireland is prospering.

It was a perfect picture that met our gaze as we looked around. The small fields were divided with thick hedges, or stone walls, sometimes with a wall of earth. Groves were frequent. Here and there a lordly mansion peered out at us through the trees.

Quite a distance to our left we could see Macroom, where the railroad from Cork ends. It looked so quiet and still in that region that morning that I was reminded that there was a tradition that the gentle Quaker, William Penn, was born there. Penn's father had a seat at Macroom, but I think the young

William gave his first cry in London. At least, I once saw the font in a London church in which he was immersed as a tiny infant.

"Now for the mountains," said Mike, as the Kerry hills drew near. Their peaks loomed up before us big as the Himalayas. Mike began to raise the airship higher and higher.

Right here I want to confess that often throughout the whole trip in this aeroplane with Mike I had shaky feelings that were a little unpleasant. Once in a while in imagination I could see myself tumbling over and over to the ground, like a wounded bird. Nor were my fears altogether groundless, as we shall see. If Mike had any such apprehensions he never said a word to me about it. I rather think he was so busily engaged constantly with the operation of the aeroplane that he had little time to think of anything else. I had much better chance to see the country than he did, but I also had more time on my hands during which I could conjure up all kinds of disasters. I well remember that, as we rose to a dizzy height, in order to clear the Kerry Mountains, I had almost a nervous attack. For a moment I shut my eyes and heartily wished I was on the earth again. If I could have gotten safely to land just then, I am afraid that all the gold in Ophir would not have tempted me to fly again. I was roused by a cry from Mike.

"Look," he fairly shouted, "isn't that grand?"

I opened my eyes quickly and saw Mike, with his face all aglow, gazing on a high peak which we soon recognized as Mount Mangerton.

It towered far above us, high as we were, for this peak is over 2,700 feet high. Soon the Devil's Punchbowl, another high mountain peak, with a flat top, came into view. This mountain, which is over 2,600 feet high, is easily recognized. Formerly it was a volcano, but long ago burnt itself out. The crater is now filled with clear, cold spring water, which is piped to the village of Killarney. It is surely an Irishism to call this beautiful water from this huge natural reservoir the "devil's punch."

We were looking so intently on these great hills that we crossed the crest of the divide before we were aware. All at once Mike startled me again.

"In the name of all that is great, look there," he exclaimed.

Never can I forget the sight that lay before us as I lowered my eyes and caught my first glimpse of the Vale of Killarney. The panorama was one of surpassing loveliness. There was no fear whatever in my heart now. All was wonder, admiration, delight. The three Killarney Lakes lay embosomed among the towering hills. The Lakes are fully eleven miles long and at one place two and a half miles broad. Magnificent forests fringe them on every side, and over sixty wooded islands float in the charmed waters. Just ahead of us was Muckross Abbey. This ancient Abbey was founded in 1440 by the McCarthys, and is a notable ruin. The walls and tower are in good condition. We could see the ivy glisten in the morning light from the top of the tower, and I caught a passing glimpse of the gigantic yew tree, nearly fourteen feet in circumference, which every visitor to Muckross Abbey will remember.

"Hurrah for old Ireland," cried Mike, as we glided down to within 150 feet of the waters of the Upper Lake. We soon rose again to about 300 feet above the water, as this gave us the best view, and at this altitude we sailed triumphantly along the entire course of the Lakes.

Here we first noticed the effect that an aeroplane had on the ordinary denizens of the earth. It was now 6:00 o'clock, and some early risers among the tourists at Killarney were enjoying the marvels of a Killarney morning along the banks. We could hear their excited exclamations as they caught sight of us, but we flew on majestically.

We soon passed the two smaller Lakes, which are joined by short narrow streams, and discerned Ross Castle clothing itself with all the glories of a morning of sunshine as it has done, every time it has had a chance, for 600 years. I say "every time it has had a chance" advisedly, for all who are acquainted with Killarney weather know that this fine ruin is often compelled to clothe itself with morning mists and rain.

Ross Castle was on our right and, beyond it, we could see Kenmare House, the home of the Earl of Kenmare, who owns Killarney. It is situated in the midst of a lovely park, with beautiful gardens, covering fully 1900 acres of woodland and lawn. However, as Mike and I sailed past it in our airship we would not have exchanged places with the Earl himself. Beyond Kenmare House we could see Killarney village straggling along amongst the trees. We were now crossing the Lower Lake, which is the largest, being nearly six miles long. We turned to our left and gazed with awe at the towering peaks which enclose this scene of beauty. The shifting of the light among the hills was glorious. Looking over our shoulders to the left we caught sight of Carntual, over 3,400 feet high, the highest mountain in Ireland. Altogether there are six prominent peaks, and as they rise from the level they make a majestic scene. We passed directly over the Innisfallen island. This large and beautiful island in the Lower Lake covers twenty-one acres and from above it looked like "a beautiful miniature of a beautiful country." We could see the famous ruins of Innisfallen Abbey on the island. This Abbey was founded in 600 by St. Finian, and it is one of the oldest ecclesiastical ruins in Erin. The Irish poet, Thomas Moore, has immortalized this little Island in his ode:

"Sweet Innisfallen, fare thee well."

After passing Innisfallen we discussed our further route. Mike wanted to circle over the Lakes again, but I objected. I wanted to carry away the remembrance of Killarney as I had seen it for the first time from an aeroplane. I was afraid a second look would take away some of the charm. Mike also wanted to go up the Gap of Dunloe, but I also objected to this, as I wished to hurry on direct to the North of Ireland that day. We compromised by agreeing to turn around at the north end of the lakes, and make a circle over the north part of Lower Lake, while we took our last look at Killarney's Vale.

When we had finally turned our backs on the glorious scene and Mike started north over the high plains, I repeated softly:

"Beauty's home, Killarney,

Heaven's reflex Killarney.

Angels fold their wings and rest

In this Eden of the West."

Mike roused me rudely from my dreams by remarking:

"These two angels haven't folded their wings from the looks of things. See how the ground flies past."

I laughed good-naturedly and gradually woke up from the spell of the beauteous Lakes of Killarney.

I pulled out my watch. It was 6:20. A short time later we caught sight of the railroad between Killarney and Tralee and followed it about 100 feet above the tracks.

Blarney Castle

CHAPTER III

OUR EXPERIENCES IN COUNTY KERRY

AS we winged our way above the railroad ties we rested after the excitement of Killarney. We were now in the heart of Kerry. This part of Ireland is not as prosperous as some other parts. The land is hilly and rocky. Fences are generally made of stone. The little cottages are also built of stone, thatched with straw. We could see the stack of peats beside them to be used as fuel, and the little potato patch which furnished food. Blue smoke was beginning to curl in the air from some of these cabins, telling us that rural Ireland was awakening for another day of life, such as it is.

Of all the sensations that ever visited Ireland, we surely were the greatest in modern times. We were much amused to see the different ways in which our appearance in the air was greeted. Sometimes the children (plentiful throughout all Ireland) would be playing in front of the cabin. As they heard the noise of our motor we could see them stop their play and gaze at us in amazement, and then, with a yell, all would dive at once for the door of their home. The mother, generally with a baby in her arms, would appear quickly. Sometimes the woman would shriek, like the children, and run inside again. At other times we noticed the women get down on their knees, as in prayer. Once or twice, the woman ran out and waved her arms at us, as though in greeting. The men generally looked stolidly at us in mute amazement.

We had an exciting time when passing a morning train coming from Tralee. We could see it smoking in the distance, and to avoid a collision, as Mike said, we turned the aeroplane about 100 feet to the right side of the track. The engineer caught sight of us first, and signalled us with a number of toots on his whistle. The tooting brought the passengers to the windows and soon heads were sticking out along the side of the train from one end to the other. They waved their hats, handkerchiefs, umbrellas, newspapers, and I saw one old gentleman vigorously shaking a book at us. I took out my handkerchief and waved it in return. The engineer kept tooting his whistle until he was far past us.

We watched the little Kerry cows, which looked carefully for any stray vegetation to be found in the Kerry uplands, for we had heard that the Kerry cow never looks up, for fear it would lose a bite. Certainly none looked up at us. Cows and men have a serious time of it in Kerry, forcing a churlish soil for daily food. Many of the men in Kerry spend part of the year in England working there, while the wives and children look after the cabbage and potato patches. We saw pigs and goats, and a few sheep around some of the cottages.

The English Government has a Board, called the Congested Districts' Board, which is at present doing excellent work in assisting the people of Kerry and others of these hilly western counties. This board aids in migration to other parts of Ireland, if it is found necessary, and also assists in developing the country as far as is possible. Breeds of stock are improved through its help, and industries, such as rug-making, lace-making and basket-making, are encouraged. This Board has also been useful in developing the fisheries industry on the west coast by constructing landing places and equipping boats for the fishermen.

As the morning advanced, and the entire population had aroused itself we were kept in a state of continual amusement by the excitement we caused, as we whizzed across the solitary moors. I felt real sympathy with Bridget, who, as she walked from the wedding altar on Pat's arm, whispered to him:

"If we could only stand and see ourselves now, wouldn't it be hivin, Pat?" I felt if we could only see ourselves from the ground and hear the comments of the natives our bliss would have been full.

We passed Tralee at 6:35. This is a pretty town situated on Tralee Bay. There are many beautiful residences in its neighborhood. Lord Kirchener was born here.

We were 200 feet in the air when we swept at full speed over the closely built houses of the town. We could see a few people stirring on the streets and they looked up at us in wonder, but did not make any manifestation. Evidently they knew what an aeroplane was.

After passing Tralee we kept close to the coast, and soon saw the wide mouth of the river Shannon ahead of us. This is Ireland's largest river, 220 miles long, pouring itself into the sea North of County Kerry. The Kerry coast is rather bleak and it was with a feeling of relief that we rushed across the wide mouth of the Shannon into County Clare.

Here our motor gave its first trouble. As we were crossing the Shannon it alarmed me by beginning to "knock" (as motorists say) and Mike told me the sparker was not working properly. We had planned to make our first landing at Kilkee on the coast of Clare, and, as this was not far distant, Mike kept on at full speed along the coast. The coast scenery here is rugged and grand. Kilkee is situated at the head of a little bay, called Moore's Bay. When we reached this bay Mike sped clear out over its waters, to my amazement, and then turned up the bay to Kilkee.

Coming up the bay we could see much excitement on the shore near the town. People were running down to the shore from all directions. Mike circled over the town, about 300 feet in the air, and then came down on a level stretch of coast beside the village.

Kilkee is over 100 miles from Cork, as the crow, or aeroplane, flies. We landed exactly at 8:00 o'clock. As I stepped from my seat, I felt stiff and lame, but a little exercise straightened me out. Mike busied himself at once with the motor. He began unscrewing the spark plugs and overhauling the whole engine.

Meanwhile the crowd kept gathering until, I suppose, in ten minutes, the entire town was standing around us open-mouthed. The boys in the crowd closed in on us at once and began asking all sorts of questions. When we told them we were from America the buzz of excitement grew louder, as they thought at first that we had crossed the Atlantic, since we came directly from the sea. Mike, at last, explained that we had only come from Cork that morning. This was wonderful enough to them and we heard all kinds of exclamations. "The Saints preserve us," said one good lady, with a shawl wrapped around her head, "what's the world coming to?"

"Begorra," said a genuine Irishman, "I never thought they could make a crow out of a man."

Some volunteered the information that they had sons, or brothers, in America, and it was not long until the crowd and us were on familiar terms. We hired two honest-looking fellows to watch the aeroplane, and keep the boys off from it, while we went down the straggling street of the town, looking for a place to get some refreshments.

A man, whom one of the bystanders assured us was "the bist man in town," took us in charge and escorted us to his own home. His good wife, a kindly, middle-aged Irish woman of the middle class, soon had a cup of hot tea and some "scones" ready for us. This was our first taste of Irish hospitality and it astonished us.

We found our host a most companionable man. When we explained our plans about an aeroplane trip all around Ireland, he said:

"You Americans can do anything."

Our host accompanied us back to the airship where there was still the same wondering crowd. The two watchmen were busy keeping the little lads away from the machine. They helped Mike arrange the starting rail, and Mike and I took our seats.

Our guards cleared the way. Mike started the motor, and shouted "Goodbye."

"Bye-bye," shouted the crowd, in the heartiest way.

"Come back again," shouted our host.

At this a little boy piped up, to the amusement of us all:

"Fly away Jack, fly away Jill;

Come back Jack, come back Jill."

Amid cheers we arose lightly from the earth, and were soon speeding once more up the Clare coast towards Galway. We left Kilkee at 9:00 o'clock.

CHAPTER IV

A THRILLING VISIT TO CONNEMARA

I had read of the grandeur of the Irish seacoast in County Clare, and I asked Mike to keep as close to the sea as he could. He obeyed me only too well, half of the time being over the ocean.

The rugged cliffs grew more and more picturesque as we neared Hag's Head. After passing over this promontory, the famous Moher Cliffs came into view. These are sheer precipices, fully 600 feet high, and, as seen from the ocean, they present a magnificent appearance. In passing these cliffs our aeroplane was about 500 feet above the sea, and about 100 feet out from land, so that we saw them to the best advantage. These cliffs stretch along the coast for five or six miles. From the Moher Cliffs we turned landward, in a northeastly direction, as we wished to pass over the city of Galway, and enter the Connemara country from the shores of Lake Corrib.

The Clare farms seemed somewhat better than those of Kerry, but not much. We saw many one-room cabins. For many miles we flew about 60 feet over Clare, and I observed the country with interest. Clare and Galway are the present centers of unrest in Ireland. There is where "cattle-driving" is practised most. Fences are destroyed and large herds of cattle, belonging to some landlord, are scattered over the country roads, The cause of "cattle-driving" is the enmity of the peasants toward the landlords who turn their estates into vast grazing farms, thus depriving the peasants of any soil to cultivate.

The Government has tried to have the landlords sell out their estates to these landless ones, but some refuse to do so, and there is no compulsory legislation at present in the matter of landlords selling to tenants.

As these landlords do not live in Ireland and have little interest in Irish people the Government is now seeking remedial legislation which will compel the landlord to sell his estate. Absentee landlordism has been Ireland's historic curse for centuries. As one Irishman expressed it: "Ireland has been *overrun* with absentee landlords."

For many years the English Government sought merely to repress the outbreaks of the dissatisfied Irish. Now, an honest attempt is being made to cure the cause of the discontent, and this accounts for these Land Laws, which have proved of such benefit already to the Emerald Isle.

Absentee landlords are hard to intimidate by popular outbreaks. On one occasion the angry tenants threatened to shoot the steward of a particularly obnoxious landlord, and the steward wrote about it to his master in England. The brave Englishman promptly replied: "Tell the tenants that no threat to shoot *you* will terrify *me*."

Irish Cabin

The humble cot beneath the Mountain side.

We reached Galway Bay shortly after ten o'clock and fifteen minutes later we were circling over the ancient city of Galway. Galway has been called a Dutch city, and its architecture, as we looked down on it, did seem more varied than the usual plain style of Irish buildings.

We created great excitement as we circled over the city at a height of 150 feet. The motor was acting a little erratic occasionally, and I wanted Mike to alight, but he disliked facing the curious crowds.

"There are lots of bogs in County Galway," he said laughingly. "We will light easy on one of them if the motor stops."

The river, connecting Lough Corrib and Galway Bay, divides the city into two parts, connected by several bridges. Crowds rushed out on the bridges as they saw us fly overhead. We could hear them cheering and some one fired off a pistol. This frightened Mike and he started toward Lough Corrib, like a wild duck which had been bombarded by a hunter.

I saw a fine old church in Galway, and I easily recognized Queen's College. It is a noble Gothic building.

This is one of the three "godless" Colleges, established in Ireland by Queen Victoria early in her reign. They are called "godless" by the Irish because they have no specific religious instruction in their curriculum. The other Queen's Colleges are located at Belfast and Cork.

We were now speeding over Lough Corrib, a large fresh-water lake, where there is excellent fishing. Mike is a keen fisherman and his teeth watered as I told him of Lough Corrib's reputation amongst the disciples of Isaac Walton.

A few miles from Galway we turned west into the heart of the far-famed Connemara country. As we swept over this part of Ireland we could see why Connemara is so celebrated. It makes a splendid panorama. There are literally hundreds of little lakes, there is grand mountain scenery, there are the heather and peat lands in abundance.

We were glad to fly over it, however, rather than live there, for the monotony and barren soil repel a man with an active mind and a good stomach.

Men were scarce, but we saw some, mostly at work in the peat lands. We caught sight of some Connemara women also, with red skirts, and Mike said he thought they were shoeless.

We went through the pass of Kylemore, called the "Gem of Connemara." Two lofty peaks rise on each side, and, in order to avoid land currents, we had to rise to a height of 500 feet in going through.

I was astonished to see in this out-of-the-way place a magnificent country home. It was surrounded with an immense garden, and the walks and drives were beautified with flaming red fuchsia hedges.

I hastily referred to my little guide book, and found it was Kylemore Castle, and that an American lady lived there. She was formerly Miss Helena Zimmerman, of Cincinnati, Ohio, but she fell from grace and is now known as the Duchess of Manchester. She must have some pangs of conscience about it, for no live American girl would live in this solitary region unless as an act of penance for her sins.

We passed close enough to Clifden, the extreme western point in Ireland, to see Clifden Castle, and also the Marconi Station. Marconi found a resting place at Clifden for the weary wireless messages after their long flight across the Atlantic, and he has a large Station here. He also found a resting place at Clifden for his weary heart, as he married Miss O'Brien, a beauty of Western Ireland.

We could hear plainly the sending of a wireless message. It was like a bombardment, report following report, like the discharge of artillery. Passing west of the Twelve Pins, a striking group of mountains, we entered County Mayo along the seacoast. Skirting Mount Muilrea, 2,685 feet high, we turned northeast to Croagh Patrick.

If Ireland's mountains were pressed out, the area of the island would be doubled. County Mayo resembles County Clare, and the stone cabins, little fields, and winding roads, are all distinctly Irish.

We were now used to the excitement caused everywhere as we whirred over the astonished peasants. One Irishman in County Mayo amused us hugely. He must have had ears like an Indian's, for he heard our motor while we were fully a mile behind him. Turning suddenly, he gave our aeroplane one long look, and then, dropping his bundle on the road, he started to run like a hare, as if to make his escape. It may have been his conscience that troubled him. Mike lowered the aeroplane until we were not more than 25 feet above him, as we shot directly over his head. Just as we passed above him he let out an unearthly shriek.

Perhaps it was a retributive act of justice, but, at any rate, a few moments later we were a good deal more scared than the Irishman.

CHAPTER V

ALMOST A DISASTER

MY hand trembles as I recall Croagh Patrick, and our flight over it. This mountain is fully 2,500 feet high, and rises abruptly from the shores of Clew Bay. In many ways it was the most attractive mountain to me in all Ireland. There is a flat plain, with some ruins, on the top of it, and in former times it was a place of great sanctity.

Saint Patrick, after whom the mountain is named, made several pilgrimages to its summit, and here St. Patrick exercised magic power for Ireland's welfare. Here is the record in the historian's own words:

"St. Patrick brought together here all the demons, toads, serpents, and other venomous creatures in Ireland and imprisoned them in a deep ravine on the sea front of the mountain, known as Lugnademon (the pit of the demons) as fast as they came in answer to his summons, and kept them safely there until he was ready to destroy them. Then, standing on the summit of the Croagh, St. Patrick, with a bell in hand, cursed them and expelled them from Ireland for ever. And every time he rang the bell thousands of toads, adders, snakes, reptiles and other noisome things went down, tumbling neck and heels after each other, and were swallowed up for ever in the sea."

As we neared Croagh Patrick I bravely asked Mike to sail over its flat top, and see this sacred spot. Mike was ready to do it in a minute. He pulled the levers and we began to ascend, while still over two miles distant from the mountain. Higher and higher we went when we reached an altitude of 2,000 feet, I could feel my heart begin to thump.

Timing himself with an accuracy, which astonished me, Mike sailed over the top of Croagh Patrick about 30 feet above the flat plain. He circled around once and we passed close beside the ruin of the ancient chapel. There is also a large Celtic Cross standing upright on the summit.

I was so glad to have old Mother Earth so near once more, that I suggested that we land. Mike was going to bring the aeroplane down when he remembered that there was no way to rig up a starting rail on the top of Croagh Patrick, and so we kept on in our flight. A minute afterwards I was sorry we did not alight, anyhow.

After his second circle around the flat plain, which is half a mile square, Mike started east, and in a couple of minutes the earth was 2,500 feet below us. The suddenness of the appearance of this vast abyss between us and land seemed even to unnerve Mike for a moment. I almost collapsed.

Then Mike did a foolish thing. He imagined he could glide down from this height, and he shut off the motor. We glided swiftly some 300 feet, and then I could feel the aeroplane begin to sink under us. What happened I do not just know. The first intimation I had of real danger was Mike's face as he quickly turned to start the motor. I could hear the big propellers whiz behind me. In starting the motor, Mike released a lever for an instant. As we were descending with lightning speed this was almost the cause of a fatal disaster. The aeroplane began to rock violently, and I was almost thrown from my seat. The accident to Orville Wright and Lieutenant Selfridge at Washington the year before flashed before my mind. I wondered if Mike could regain control of the machine. I caught the sides of my seat and braced myself against the foot-rail. Even then I had difficulty in holding on. I glanced at Mike. His face was pale. His eyes shone. Every muscle and nerve was tense. He was like a rider on a runaway horse, determined to assert his mastery. His self-control was perfect.

In spite of Mike's coolness I am surprised we escaped. As the aeroplane kept sinking and rocking like a ship in a storm, I closed my eyes and resigned myself to my fate. I was aroused by Mike's voice.

"A close call, Jack, old boy," he said affectionately. I could see that there were tears in his eyes. He was thinking of me and of my escape. Brave Mike. I wanted to hug him right there. I looked around and saw we were about 500 feet above ground, the aeroplane gliding smoothly through the air.

It was fortunate for us there was no breeze to speak of. All that morning, except for a little while on the seacoast, the wind gave us no trouble.

I was glad to see Westpoint a few miles ahead, as we had planned to stop there for a lunch, and to replenish our supply of gasoline, or petrol, as they call it in Ireland.

One good thing came out of our Croagh Patrick experience. I began to help Mike in operating the aeroplane. I took entire charge of the motor, which I could reach more readily than he could, at any rate. This left him free to manage the levers. He was the captain and gave all orders, but I started and stopped the motor the rest of our trip.

I found this of advantage to me, especially after the rapid descent from Croagh Patrick, as it gave me something to do, and, when not engaged watching the scenery, or consulting my map or guide-book, I could busy myself with the motor.

We had other exciting incidents, but this division of labor assisted us in keeping the aeroplane completely under our control—as long as the motor worked.

CHAPTER VI

FROM WESTPOINT TO ENNISKILLEN

MIKE made an excellent landing in an open space in a beautiful park beside Westpoint. A small crowd soon gathered around us when we lit, but Mike and I paid little attention to them. I stepped out on the ground and looked at my watch. It was one o'clock. We had been in the air four hours. Mike felt the strain of this long aerial journey also, but not so much as I did. He was more accustomed to aeroplaning.

Our motor had been acting well, on the whole. It was a new style motor, without carburetor, and I had been suspicious of it, but it surpassed any motor I had ever seen in reliability.

We had just finished stretching out our tired limbs when a middle-aged man, with a kindly, honest face, but an important air, came hurrying along the driveway of the park in our direction.

We heard several in the crowd exclaim: "The Keeper, the Keeper." The new comer looked at us in astonishment and then he inspected our aeroplane. Then he looked at us again, and exclaimed: "By the Powers."

We did not know what kind of a salutation this might be, but Mike told what we were doing and why we had alighted in the Park.

The "Keeper," as they called him, at once became friendly and introduced himself as the Steward of the Marquis of Sligo, in whose park we had alighted and whose mansion was close at hand. The Steward resided at the mansion, as the Marquis did not spend much time on his Irish estate.

He invited us to come up to the mansion, which invitation we gladly accepted. Following the Steward, we soon arrived at the stately home of the Marquis of Sligo, who owns the greater part of this section of Ireland. He is an absentee landlord, but he comes to Westpoint occasionally, and he treats his tenants liberally, for an Irish landlord. The large park around his mansion is open to all Westporters. We noticed, from the signs, that automobiles were not allowed to enter the park, but aeroplanes were not excluded, at least, not yet.

The Steward served us a good lunch, and sent a boy with a pony-cart to town to get the petrol. The Sligo Mansion is luxuriously furnished, and Mike and I felt like royal travellers.

The Steward's kindness was explained when he began to talk about America. He had two brothers in the New World, and told us that tens of thousands of Irishmen from County Mayo and County Galway had left Ireland for America in the past twenty years.

Westport is the most westerly town in Ireland, and is only 1,600 miles from Nova Scotia. At one time it was proposed to run a line of steamers from here to America, but the project fell through.

We would like to have spent a day or two around Westport, but we still thought we could reach the Giant's Causeway that evening, although I was beginning to think that Antrim was quite a long ways off.

The Steward showed us around the gardens and grounds, and even offered to drive us over the town, but we were anxious to get started in the air again and we declined. It was 2:00 o'clock when we had the starting rail in place and had everything in readiness for another flight.

An immense crowd had gathered around the aeroplane. They made few remarks, evidently restrained by the presence of the steward, for whom they showed much respect. One or two did volunteer an Irish farewell.

"Ah, then," said one old woman, "it's not often we have the blessing of such fine company, good luck to your honors, and God send you safe back again."

"Good-bye," said a good-natured Son of Erin, with the map of Ireland all over his face. "Good-bye, and I hope ye can *kape on your feet* until you land agin."

"God bless you, sors," said the Steward, "and keep you safe and bring you back."

One gets used to hearing the name of Deity in Ireland, but it does not shock you. The Irish use God's name familiarly, but reverently; not lightly, as in France; or vulgarly, as so often in America. No one calls on God to damn you in Ireland. God is appealed to for blessing.

"Good-bye," Mike and I shouted, as we rose in the air. The crowd broke out in cheers, as we sailed away toward County Sligo.

We crossed several lakes and much enjoyed the rest of our flight over County Mayo, but it is not a desirable part of Ireland in which to till the soil. We passed over a pretty little town on a railroad, called Castlebar. We entered County Sligo near Swinford.

Just after entering County Sligo, Mike said to me:

"Where's our sunshine?"

I looked around. The entire sky was overcast. We were having the usual experience with the Irish weather, which some one has said is as changeable as the Irish character. Smiles and tears come at a moment's notice.

The clouds soon got to work and it began to drizzle. Passing over Sligo we could see the farms improve, and when we reached County Leitrim, which we entered near Lake Allen, we could see a marked improvement. The soil was fertile, the farms and houses were larger, and there was a general air of prosperity apparent.

Our aeroplane whizzed through the misty, rainy atmosphere, like an ocean liner through a fog, but as the upper plane got soaked through, it began to leak down on us, and the water-logged planes made the machine more difficult to control. Mike told me that the airship was not built for Irish weather, but he afterwards remedied this defect, as we shall see.

When we reached County Fermanagh we began to realize Ireland's agricultural possibilities. Ulster is a different world from Connaught. The landscape is rolling, covered with cultivated farms. The houses are often two-storied, slated, and neatly kept. There are large barns and every appearance of prosperity. The picture presented to us in Ulster was not so romantic as in Connemara, but it is more like living. In many parts of Connaught a crow would need to have its rations along, but there are signs of plenty in Ulster. We could well understand why the Irish did not altogether approve of the grim Oliver's dictum: "To Connaught with every Irishman."

The inhabitants of the North of Ireland are also different from the Irish of the West. They are largely Protestant in religion and of Scotch descent. Their forefathers were brought to Ireland by James I., in the early part of the 17th century. Several of the English rulers had a good deal to do with the history of Ireland. Henry VIII., Queen Elizabeth, Oliver Cromwell, and James I., had extensive real estate dealings in the Emerald Isle in years gone by, and when they had completed their bargains the map of Ireland was altered and the feelings of many of the Irish were badly lacerated. It has taken centuries for these wounded feelings to heal.

It was after four o'clock when we sighted the chimneys of Enniskillen. This prosperous town is built on Lake Erne, or Lough Erne, as the natives call it. Lough Erne is another of Ireland's large fresh-water lakes. Enniskillen is famous as the city which, like Londonderry endured victoriously a siege in 1689, the year of the commotion between James II. and William III. Its defenders manifested the greatest bravery. The banners captured at the Battle of the Boyne, where William III. defeated James II., hang in Enniskillen's Town Hall.

Tired and wet, I seconded heartily Mike's suggestion that we spend the night here. I felt that I could not fly another mile. We came down rather abruptly in a field near town. The water-soaked aeroplane had become hard to control, and we narrowly missed a big hawthorn hedge. A farm house was near by, and the farmer came running to us, followed by a little crowd of children of all ages. After explanations, we turned the aeroplane over to him for the night, and trudged into town. Walking seemed pleasant to us both, as we had been flying for a whole day. In spite of the misty rain, we enjoyed every step of our mile walk to the Royal Hotel. We had a good Irish supper, or "tea," as they called it, and soon afterwards we retired for the night.

The day ended perhaps a little ingloriously, but we were well content.

CHAPTER VII

A DAY IN ENNISKILLEN

WHEN we woke up late the next morning the sun was shining in at the windows. We congratulated ourselves on having escaped the bad weather of the previous evening, and we expected to again enjoy the sight of Ireland's green fields lit up with sunshine.

When I arose I felt quite stiff and sore, and I saw Mike moved around with more than his usual precision. The prolonged flight of the previous day had wearied us considerably. Some aeronauts may wonder we could make such a long flight, but straight, cross-country aeroplaning differs much from circling a mile track. The aeroplane is not so comfortable as a dirigible balloon, and a flight like Count Zeppelin's recent cross-country trip in Europe would be quite strenuous in the heavier-than-air machines at present. But a journey of 300 or 400 miles a day, with proper stops, does not call for any extraordinary endurance.

As we came down stairs to breakfast we heard a band out on the street and we noticed an air of excitement on every hand. We thought, at first, that we were the occasion of the evident agitation, but a waiter soon showed us that there were greater things, even, than aeroplanists in Ireland on that day.

"It's a foine Twelfth of July," he said to us.

"What about the Twelfth of July?" asked Mike.

The waiter stared at him, until Mike went on:

"What's going on here today?"

Then the waiter, seeing we were ignorant Americans explained to us how they celebrated the victory of the Boyne every Twelfth of July, and how the celebration that day was to be the biggest ever held. Then I remembered how the great day in the North of Ireland is the Twelfth of July, just as the Seventeenth of March is the great day in the rest of Ireland. However, St. Patrick's Day is now generally observed in some way not only in Ireland, but in all the world.

"Mike," said I, "let us stay in Enniskillen today and celebrate."

"We'll stay and rest," said Mike, "and see what they do here on the 'glorious Twelfth', as our waiter calls it."

After breakfast we went out on the streets, and found them filling up with a holiday crowd. I was reminded of a celebration of July Fourth in America. Excursion trains coming in from different points in the surrounding territory added to the crowd every hour. These excursion parties brought with them in every case one or two fife bands, and occasionally a brass band. These bands played popular airs to the great delight of the crowd. All these numerous bands, and the immense crowd of Irishmen and Irish women, gathered in a large field beside Enniskillen. It was a scene of the greatest enthusiasm. Bands in different parts of the field were playing different airs. All was hub-bub and excitement. There were stands all around where all kinds of drinks were sold. Already several plainly showed that they had been drinking a liquid much stronger than lemonade. Lads and lasses were walking around, jostling, crowding and laughing. It was a good-natured crowd, as there was no counter-demonstration of any kind, as happens sometimes in other parts of Ireland, I understand. The differences between the Roman Catholic and Protestant are very acute in the Emerald Isle for several reasons. Often the two sides have bitter disputes. In this controversy, as in all else, the inevitable humor of the Irish sometimes crops out. The famous Father O'Leary had a polemical contest with the Protestant Bishop of Cloyne. The Bishop, in a pamphlet, inveighed with great acrimony against the doctrines of the Roman Catholic Church, and particularly against purgatory.

Father O'Leary, in his reply, slyly observed, "that, much as the Bishop disliked purgatory, he might go farther and fare worse."

When Dean Swift was at Carlow, he found the Episcopal Church badly dilapidated. "Why don't you give it to the Catholics?" said the caustic Dean. "You know they would repair it and *you could take it from them afterwards.*" It is not theology alone that separates Catholics and Protestants in Ireland. The real estate deals of the English Kings and Queens have something to do with it.

We enjoyed immensely our day in Enniskillen. We saw a typical North of Ireland crowd, heard an Irish orator declaim against "the foes of Ireland," listened to Irish bands, and shared in the enthusiasm of the occasion. There was an excursion steamer running on Lough Erne and in the afternoon we had a delightful boat ride. In the evening, while at supper, we had a sample of real Irish wit. There was a large sign in the dining room with this notice: "Strangers are requested not to give any money to the waiters, as attention is charged for in the bill."

Our waiter saw Mike reading this sign, and remarked to him:

"Oh, Mister, sure that doesn't concern you at all. *We're not makin' a stranger o' you, sor.*"

We laughed heartily, and told him we never felt more at home in our lives. "Tips" are as necessary in Ireland, even when traveling with an aeroplane, as raincoats.

We had been informed that we would find wretched hotels in Ireland, but the Imperial Hotel at Cork and the Royal Hotel at Enniskillen, are excellent hotels, and, as a rule, we found the hotel accommodations satisfactory. In the evening, before dark, we sauntered forth, and Mike went into a "shop," as they call stores in Erin, and bought out their entire supply of light oil-cloth. Taking this with us, we went out to see our aeroplane. In the excitement of July Twelfth, the news of our strange craft evidently did not spread very wide, and we were very glad to escape notoriety in Enniskillen. We found the airship just as we left it the previous night. The farmer wondered what had become of us. Mike got some tacks and a hammer, and covered the upper plane entirely with oil-cloth.

"Even an airship needs a rain-coat in this country," said Mike to the farmer.

"But, sor," said the farmer, "it's such a gentle rain we have here."

The oil-cloth was quite a good idea on the part of Mike. It gave us both a big umbrella during the rest of our trip, and the sudden showers were not so disagreeable.

The next morning we started at 5:00 o'clock, and after rewarding our farmer friend for his care of the aeroplane, we ascended into the Irish atmosphere again. After circling over Enniskillen, we turned North, and, leaving Lough Erne far to the West, we sped, like a gigantic eagle, towards Tyrone.

CHAPTER VIII

CIRCLING OVER LONDONDERRY IN AN AEROPLANE

WE were almost an hour in reaching Omagh, the county seat of County Tyrone. As we flew over the city we were surprised to see how new-looking it was in appearance, as it is one of Ireland's oldest towns. I learned later that the old town had been destroyed some two hundred years ago, and that Omagh of today is comparatively modern. It is a neat and prosperous city, with streets, some of them very steep, running in every direction. A beautiful Cathedral adorns the hillside, and an old barracks, now used as a police station, is an imposing structure. There are several large Presbyterian churches which show every sign of progress and prosperity. There were only a few people on the streets when we winged our way across the city at 6:00 o'clock. These stared up at us and we could see them running to the high places to keep us in sight. The farms in County Tyrone looked large compared with the microscopic farms of Connaught and Kerry, but they looked very small to an American. The macadamized roads are models in the way they are kept up, but they are narrow and winding. When the wagon roads cross a railroad, there is never a grade crossing. Generally the wagon road runs over the railroad, but occasionally dips under it.

LONDONDERRY, IRELAND.

We had another exciting experience with an early train from Omagh to Derry. We caught up with this train at Newtonstewart, a picturesque little place. The engineer saw us, and, like his fellow-Irishman in County Kerry, he tooted his whistle in our honor. We flew alongside the train for several miles, about 100 feet from the side of the track, and 30 feet high in the air. As the race continued, every passenger grew more and more excited. They cheered and shouted. Mike, with both his hands on his levers, could only look down and grin, but I was able to wave my handkerchief and cap. The engineer gave one long, farewell toot, as he stopped at a station, while we flew on our way.

At Strabane, a good-sized town, some twenty miles from Londonderry, we created wild excitement. A number of people were around the station, as we whizzed past, just about 20 feet in the air, directly over the railroad tracks. We rose to a height of 75 feet just after passing the station, and we could hear their loud cheering, as we rose like a bird. The river Foyle formed at Strabane by the junction of the rivers Finn and Mourne, flows from Strabane to Derry (as Londonderry is called by the natives) a wide and noble stream.

Mike turned the aeroplane directly over the river after we left Strabane, and we flew above it for many miles. This Foyle Valley is a rich agricultural country, and I could see the crops of oats, flax, turnips, and potatoes, growing in luxuriance in the fertile little fields. About half way between Strabane and Derry our motor gave us the first serious trouble. While we were sailing along over the river, all at once it stopped, like a balky horse.

"Start the motor, Jack," Mike yelled, thinking I had shut her off.

"It stopped itself," I answered.

"Gee-whitaker," said Mike, and I could see him tug at the levers in order to turn the airship towards the shore and bring it safely to the ground. Fortunately we were quite high in the air, fully 200 feet, and we were only a short distance from the east bank of the river. In a few seconds Mike had brought us down safely, a few yards from the river's edge, on the flat embankment. Mike soon remedied the trouble—a screw had loosened. How to get started again was now our problem, as we needed some kind of starting rail. Some men around a group of houses a short distance away, saw us, and came running with all speed. They stared and gaped at us without saying a word. Mike spoke to one of them, and explaining our trouble, asked him to get a long stout board, to use as a starting rail. The rustic ran back to the cottages, and soon returned with a good board, which Mike soon turned into a starting rail. Meanwhile, his companions began to make remarks, in true Irish style, about the aeroplane.

"Isn't that a new way to '*hoof it*?'" said a fellow with an Irish cast of countenance.

"Let us get one, and then we can fly to America," said one of the youngest of them, a lad about eighteen years of age. The young fellows in rural Ireland all look upon America as the Eldorado of the world.

One of them said to me: "I should think, sor, your air-boat would be lonesome in Ireland."

"Why?" I asked.

"Because," said Erin's son, "it's the only one in the whole country, sor."

"Come back again, sors," one of them shouted as we arose from the earth to continue our journey. We noticed this is a familiar parting phrase in Erin.

It was seven o'clock when we saw the smoke of Derry. In spite of our recent mishaps, Mike steered right into the middle of the Foyle, as we came close to the city. At Derry the river is spanned by a fine iron bridge. As we passed over this bridge, about twenty feet above it, we frightened a passing horse into a runaway, and attracted the attention of a crowd of laborers, who were crossing the bridge. Speeding on down the Foyle, we saw below us the masts and funnels of a number of ships, for Derry is an important seaport. Along the docks crowds of working men greeted us with shouts, and some of the steamers sent us a scream of whistles. I was much interested in old Derry. I had visited it often before, and, when we reached the end of the docks, I asked Mike to circle clear around the city. We rose to a height of 300 feet, and the famous city lay under us, like a picture. We could see the historic walls which enclosed the ancient city, about a mile in circumference, and still adorned with many antique cannon. The well-remembered siege of Derry happened in 1689, when James II. besieged the city for 105 days, and the gallant defenders were reduced to the greatest extremities. To make matters worse, Colonel Lundy, who commanded the garrison, turned traitor, and opened negotiations with the besiegers. His treachery was discovered, and he made his escape in disguise. Rev. Geo. Walker, one of the heroes of the siege, has been remembered with a fine monument, built on one of the bastions of the wall. On this monument, every December 18th, an effigy of the traitor, Lundy, is burned amid great cheering by the descendants of the old defenders of Derry. Derry Cathedral has interesting relics of this famous siege, but it is not a noteworthy building from an architectural viewpoint.

Derry is now quite an educational centre. Foyle College is a prosperous institution with a pleasant location, overlooking the river. Magee College, a Presbyterian institution, is beautifully located on a high hill north of the city. The architecture of the building is stately, and this seat of learning is an important part of modern Derry. A large number of the Irish Presbyterian ministers are educated here.

We could see the large shirt factories, which bring much wealth, and lots of women into Derry. Most of the employees are women.

The town on the east side of the Foyle is called Waterside. There is a high bluff, just south of Waterside, which is covered with villas owned by prosperous Derrymen. We passed over a large military barracks at the north end of Waterside. Evidently, some of the officers in the barracks had been watching our flight around the city, and they were ready for us. As we swept over the barrack square, three large guns were suddenly discharged, in our honor, we suppose. Mike was so astonished at the sudden reports that he unconsciously pulled a lever, making the aeroplane veer sharply so that it began to rock. He had it under control again in a moment, but we could hear the cheering of the red-coated soldiers, as they noticed our maneuvers.

We sailed on, sorry to leave the historic Maiden City (as Derry is proudly called because it was never captured.) Shortly after passing the barracks, we turned east, sailing over a number of delightful country homes. Two miles east of Derry we passed over the lovely valley of the Faughan river. This beautiful spot was one of the finest scenes we found in the whole north of Ireland. It was a valley filled with peace, quietness and sunshine that morning. We went as far east as Dungiven, a small country town about the centre of County Derry. Many modern mansions adorn the countryside, and the fertile soil well repays its careful cultivation.

"Look at the rain," said Mike, as we turned north from Dungiven.

And raining it was. While I was gazing down on Derry's green fields and lovely rivers, the clouds were hastily gathering overhead, and threatening all kinds of things. Soon the rain was pattering down upon our aeroplane, but it fell harmlessly on our rain-coated airship. It was only a shower, but while it lasted the rain came down in a hurry. As an Irishman would put it, some of the drops were "as big as a shilling or eighteen pence." In a little while the sudden tempest had spent itself, and the sun was shining as though nothing had happened.

We followed a small stream, called the Roe, to Limavady, which we reached a little after eight o'clock. We had planned to stop here for some refreshments for ourselves, and our faithful "bird," and Mike was delighted to see a large level field near the town, where he made a good descent, alighting without a jar. In five minutes, people were running towards us in all directions. We had circled the little town before alighting, and had aroused everybody. They crowded around us as at Kilkee, and soon began asking all kinds of questions. We satisfied them as best we could, hired a watchman to guard the aeroplane, and, accompanied by a motley following, we walked into Limavady.

CHAPTER IX

ALIGHTING AT THE GIANT'S CAUSEWAY

WE ascended from Limavady at 8:30. We were once more cheered to the echo as we left the earth. After leaving Limavady, we came to a low range of hills, and Mike had to use his raising levers freely as we climbed their sides. We saw the familiar heather and peat, and even the little cabins, much the same as we saw in County Mayo. At the top of the hills we had a magnificent view. We could see Coleraine clearly, nestling beside the Bann river, and, away in the distance, we saw again the sea. The surrounding country was like a panorama. We glided swiftly down the mountain side, and flew around the quaint old town of Coleraine. Scotch-Irishmen live in Coleraine, and it has the reputation of having the best bakers in the whole island. Mike and I did not condescend to test this, although it was perhaps as well for us not to alight there, for Coleraine is famous for something besides bread. Fine old Coleraine whisky is known throughout the length and breadth of Ireland. A Donegal clergyman, on hearing of a sermon against drink, said: "Sure, I am forever at them about it. It's the bad stuff they take that does the mischief. I have told them from the altar that I never touched a drop myself *but the best Coleraine.*"

Sky-pilots, whether spiritual or atmospheric, have to leave whisky alone nowadays, so, in spite of its fame, we merely circled over the city. Coleraine is known for many centuries in Irish history. St. Patrick built a church here. Columba visited it in 590. Later on the salmon fishing in the river Bann, which flowed through the city, made Coleraine a place of some commercial importance. Like Derry and Enniskillen, Coleraine was besieged in 1689 by the troops of James II., and the garrison was compelled to evacuate the town, and retreat to Derry.

After passing over Coleraine, we came to the seacoast again at Portstewart. I could see the row of houses along the quay, in one of which Lever used to live. Lever's home was in Dublin, but he spent a year as a dispensary doctor at Portstewart, and did some writing here. A stiff breeze was blowing along the coast, and Mike was kept busy handling the airship. Leaving Portstewart, we went along the rough coast to Portrush. This was formerly a dreaded coast, many a brave ship going to pieces on the rocks. Portrush is the fashionable watering place of the North of Ireland, and it is crowded with visitors during July and August. The town is built on a ridge that projects into the sea. The strands are beautiful. The ridge on which the town is built ends in a hill, called Ramore hill, which is a favorite promenade. We could see the bathers swimming in the surf, as we skimmed along the strand towards the White Rocks. These are cliffs of a strange white formation. A little beyond the White Rocks Mike slowed up, and passed around the picturesque ruins of Dunluce Castle. This ancient ruin crowns a high cliff, and, before men could fly, was a difficult place to reach. Right in front of us we could see the headlands above the Giant's Causeway. I did not very much enjoy my sail from Dunluce to those headlands. After leaving the Castle, Mike turned directly out to sea, instead of following the coast, and crossed a bay of a few miles to the Causeway. I remembered our experience over the river Foyle, and I did not altogether appreciate Mike's daring. I was really relieved as we rose over the great cliff that over-hangs the Causeway, and circled around with the earth under us. We were both delighted to reach the Northern end of the Island. It was not quite ten o'clock when we arrived.

There are two large hotels on the high cliff, and we could see the tourists, many with field glasses, watching us in the air. Mike, in the exuberance of his joy and self-confidence, made three great circles before landing. In making the last circle he went out over the sea again, and then alit beside the Railroad hotel as lightly as a bird could have done. The crowd cheered us as we stepped out, and some of the men came forward to shake hands and congratulate us. We were asked if we were the Wright Brothers, and when we said we were not, some of them suggested Curtiss, Farnam, and other well-known aeronauts. When we explained we were simply tourists, using the latest and best way of travel, they looked at each other, and when Mike told how we had come from Cork, they laughed outright. I do not believe half a dozen in the crowd thought we had come any further than from Portrush. I expect they would not have believed we could fly at all had they not seen us alight.

One Englishman laughed so contemptuously that I noticed Mike looked at him in disgust.

"It reminds me of the Manager of the Chicago Stockyards," said the Englishman.

"Why, what about the Manager of the Chicago Stockyards?" asked Mike hotly.

Not noticing Mike's rising temper, the Englishman went on to tell of a couple of Irishmen who went to Chicago, and while there, visited the Stockyards. One of the managers noticed the interest Erin's sons took in the great institution, and thought he would play a joke. Pointing to a large herd of cattle, which were being driven into one of the lower buildings, the Manager called attention to them, and when the last tail had disappeared, he waited a few moments and then pulled a great freight elevator rope and down came a large elevator loaded with canned meat.

"There," said the Manager, slyly winking at an employee near by, "there are all those cows you saw, hides, horns, hoofs, and every thing, all canned and ready for market. Did you ever see anything like that in Ireland, Pat?" he asked.

Pat at once took out his note book and began to write. The Manager looked over Pat's shoulder and read on Pat's note book: "The Manager of the Chicago Stockyards is the biggest liar I have met yet."

Mike was furious as he heard the crowd join in uproarious laughter at our expense.

"Do you call me a liar, sir," said Mike, squaring himself in front of the joking Englishman.

The Englishman was taken aback at Mike's earnestness, and, not knowing what to say, merely laughed in a foolish kind of way.

"I allow no man to call me a liar," said Mike, as he stepped closer to his antagonist. Mike was a Yankee, but I knew there was Irish blood in his veins, and this rash Englishman had aroused him.

I was afraid our aeroplane trip was going to end in a fiasco, when something altogether unexpected happened.

"I believe you, sir," said a sweet, charming, musical voice, "and you must tell us all about your wonderful voyage over Ireland. It must have been delightful."

Mike turned to see the speaker, and, in a moment, every trace of anger left his face, and he stood like a blushing schoolboy.

At the same time a dark-haired, rosy-cheeked girl, of nineteen or twenty, clad in a dainty white sailor dress and cap came forward, holding out her hand.

Mike recovered himself, clasped her hand, saying: "I thank you, Miss—."

"Edith O'Neill," added the girl.

"I am glad to meet you, Miss O'Neill," said Mike, and I never saw him look more manly.

The crowd burst into applause, and all was good cheer again. That was the first meeting of Mike and Miss O'Neill, and it was fraught with more meaning than any of us thought at the time. I found out later in the day that Miss O'Neill was a descendant of the famous Irish O'Neill family. Her father was a wealthy Dublin lawyer, and she and her parents were taking a short holiday at the Causeway.

After seeing that the aeroplane was carefully stored away in a corner of the hotel yard, Mike and I retired to our room until lunch. Mike was in splendid humor, and he had every reason to be. Our aeroplane trip was a success. We had conquered the Irish air. An Irish heiress is still more difficult to conquer, but it is wonderful what one can do in the Irish atmosphere.

CHAPTER X

OUR REST ON THE ANTRIM COAST

WHEN we came down to the noon lunch at the hotel, we met Miss O'Neill and a fine-looking, elderly gentleman and lady, whom she at once introduced as her parents.

Mr. O'Neill was very cordial, and invited us to sit at their table. In some way I managed to monopolize both Mr. and Mrs. O'Neill, leaving Mike out in the cold with Miss O'Neill. However, I don't think he minded it in the least, as both he and the fair Irish girl seemed to get on good terms at once. I was surprised at Mike. I had never known him before to take an interest in any girl. He always had avoided the young ladies as long as I had known him. I think it must have been the Irish atmosphere.

After lunch Mr. O'Neill and I went for a walk over the Causeway. Mrs. O'Neill took an afternoon nap, and so Mike and Miss Edith were left alone together again.

One reason why Mike capitulated so easily to the charms of this fair Irish maiden was that she had been an ardent student of aeronautics, and was even ambitious to fly herself.

During the afternoon Mr. O'Neill showed me the wonders of the Giant's Causeway. It is no wonder that this unique phenomenon in geology is so far-famed. A stream of lava, 2600 feet wide, and fifteen miles long, instead of forming the usual basaltic rock when it had cooled, formed itself into detached columns, from six to thirty feet long, and from eight to twenty-four inches in diameter. These strange columns, mostly pentagonal or hexagonal in formation, present a smooth surface in three parallel terraces along this Antrim coast and make the most remarkable natural pavement ever seen by the eyes of man. There are forty thousand of these columns, and every one of them is a perfect geometrical figure. The columns are so close together that water will not pass between them, and yet each is separate.

"With skill so like, yet so surpassing art;

With such design, so just in every part,

That reason ponders, doubtly if it stand

The work of mortal or immortal hand."

As we walked over this marvelous piece of rock formation, Mr. O'Neill told me the legend of Finn McCool, and how he built the Causeway over to

Scotland, in order to provide a way for Ben Donner to come over to Ireland to accept his challenge. Ben was the champion of Scotland, as Finn was in Ireland, and Finn was determined to see which was the better man. In the contest Finn was victorious, and as there was no further use for this strange roadway across the sea, most of it had been swept away, but a little was left on the Antrim coast, a relic of Finn's remarkable handiwork.

HORIZONTAL PILLARS, GIANT'S CAUSEWAY.

HORIZONTAL PILLARS, GIANT'S CAUSEWAY.

Science attempts to explain the Causeway by saying that, when the rock was in a fluid state, crystalization set in, and produced the phenomenon. It is claimed that the Palisades of the Hudson are a somewhat similar formation. On account of the fact that rocks do not naturally crystalize, however, the Causeway still remains the puzzle of the scientist.

The scenery along the coast near the Causeway is sublime, and there is a walk along the face of the cliff, which I found almost as dangerous as aeroplaning. I found Mr. O'Neill a charming companion, and I thoroughly enjoyed his society. After we had talked of the Causeway, our conversation drifted to the subject of Ireland's history. Naturally, this was a subject dear to his heart. He gave me a brief epitome of Irish history which was new to me. Irish history begins with St. Patrick in the fifth century of our era. St. Patrick evangelized the Irish, and, as a result of his labors, Ireland was the land of saints and scholars during the period between the sixth and tenth centuries. The Danes, who settled around the coasts of Ireland, broke up this peaceful prosperity. Schools were demolished and the students scattered. Brian Boru brought back a brief period of glory to Irish history by uniting the Irish under his able sway. He defeated the Danes in a decisive battle at Clontarf, near Dublin, in 1014, but he lost his life at the close of that fatal day. Ireland was left rudderless again. The petty chiefs quarrelled amongst themselves, and in 1170 the English came over and claimed Ireland. The struggles of the Irish for political freedom have been pathetic. The native Irish were often treated as the Indians were by the white men in America, but with this vital exception. In America the Indian quietly died out, and gave not trouble. In Ireland, the Irish lived, multiplied, and filled Ireland with Irishmen. The real estate deals made in Irish land by several of England's rulers left a bad taste in the mouths of the Irish. In 1641, taking advantage of England's Civil War, the Irish rose against the English and Scotch colonists in Ireland with terrible fury. In 1649 Cromwell reduced Ireland again to English rule, treating the natives with savage ferocity. Another rebellion arose in 1689, when James II. was driven from the English throne by William III. James came to Ireland and the Irish rose in his favor. William III. again conquered the Irish. Thus the history has gone on. Laws of fearful severity were enacted, and the native Irish, for almost a century, were outcasts in the land of their forefathers.

Mr. O'Neill was a great admirer of Daniel O'Connell. He told me that a new era began for Ireland when Daniel O'Connell, with the assistance of English statesmen, took off some of Ireland's heaviest burdens. "I believe," said Mr. O'Neill, with great earnestness, "that since Gladstone's time, England has been trying to do justice to Ireland."

He assured me that the Irish had never acknowledged that England had conquered them. He told me about an English schoolboy who was asked to write an essay on the "Conquest of Ireland," and he began: "The Conquest of Ireland began in 1170, and is still going on."

I was much impressed with the way O'Neill recited to me the history of his country. Sometimes tears came into his eyes. He quoted, with much feeling, a few lines from an Irish poet:

"Of old the harp of Innisfail

Was turned to gladness,

But, Oh! how oft it's told a tale

Of wide prevailing sadness."

He expressed high hopes that Ireland's darkest days are past. He believes all Irishmen in Ireland today, the Protestant in the North and the Catholic in the South, should blot out the unhappy memories of the past centuries, and forget the mistakes of former times, and face the future, united in honest efforts for Ireland's welfare.

As we walked along, while he told me all this, we suddenly came upon Mike and Edith at the Giant's Wishing Chair. This is a place where the columns of the Causeway are arranged something like a rude chair, and it is said if you sit in this "chair," and wish, that your wish will come true. When we came on the scene Edith was sitting in the chair, wishing. Mike was standing by her side, evidently much amused.

"What's your wish," Mike asked, after we had joined them.

"I wished that I might fly tomorrow," she answered with a blush. Then, walking up to her father she said:

"Oh, Papa, can I take a ride in the aeroplane with Mr. Connor tomorrow?"

I saw Mr. Neill glance quickly at her flushed face, and then turn away with a sigh. She was his only child.

"Why, why," he answered, "what put such a notion as that in your head? Did you, sir?" and he looked accusingly at Mike.

"No, sir," said Edith, before Mike could speak, "Mr. Connor never said a word to me about it."

"We'll see tomorrow," said her father.

"I think my wish will come true," I heard Miss O'Neill say to Mike, as they walked ahead of us up the rough road to the hotel.

I did not hear Mike's reply but it seemed to please her immensely.

I resumed my talk with Mr. O'Neill about Ireland. I asked him about recent land laws. I found him enthusiastic about the Wyndham Act of 1903, providing for the purchase of their farms by Irish tenants.

"It means a new Ireland inside a generation," he earnestly exclaimed. He then went on to say that the Irish people as a whole, the native Celt, the descendants of the Scotch, English and French, were developing a distinctive modern Irish race, which would be able to hold its own in every department of life. This led him to speak of the Irish people in America, and I found he had followed the fortunes of his countrymen across the sea. He was delighted when I told him that Mike and I were Irish Yankees.

"County Antrim ought to be a sacred place to you," he said to me, "for two of your great Presidents traced their ancestry to Antrim." He went on to tell me that President Jackson's father sailed from Carrickfergus, near Belfast, in 1765, going to North Carolina. He also told me that the great-great-grandfather of President McKinley emigrated from Conagher, County Antrim, in 1743. He had himself seen the old McKinley homestead. Mr. O'Neill and I were on such good terms of real friendship that very evening, that I could hardly believe it possible I had only met him that day. I believe it was the Irish atmosphere.

CHAPTER XI

A FLIGHT IN AN AEROPLANE WITH AN IRISH GIRL

NEXT morning at breakfast Miss O'Neill again asked her father's permission to ascend in the aeroplane with Mike. I assured him that if Mike promised to go over land there was absolutely no danger, for, as I put it: "Mr. Connor can alight as easily as a crow."

"But what if he were to alight on a tree?" he asked with a twinkle in his eye, which showed me that Mike and Miss O'Neill were going to fly together all right.

At last, the father gave his consent, but warned Mike not to go out over the sea. It was arranged that they should ascend at 10:00 o'clock.

Mike had to make a trip to Portrush to get some petrol, and he decided to take Miss O'Neill along with him on that journey.

"Can she take such a long trip on her first flight?" I asked, remembering my own experiences.

"Jack," said Mike, confidently, "she can beat you now as an aeronaut. She knows all about it already. I am sure she will have no trouble."

We fixed up a starting rail in the sloping field in front of the hotel, and at 10:00 o'clock Miss Edith and her father and mother appeared.

Word had gotten out about the trip and every tourist around the Causeway was gathered in the field to see the ascent.

Edith was a perfect picture. Not having an airship dress, she had arranged herself in closely fitting riding habit. She made a few necessary changes, and the dress was adapted well for her unique excursion. She wore a blue sailor cap, matching her dress, and also a pair of blue gloves.

As Mike was assisting her into the aeroplane, I heard a lady exclaim, "What a pretty blue-bird." I could not help thinking that a fairer bird than Miss Edith never flew beneath the kindly Irish skies.

It was a perfect day, and there was a very slight breeze.

After seeing that Edith was seated, Mike vaulted easily into his seat.

"All ready," he shouted, as he started the motor. "Good-bye," said Edith to us all, as the aeroplane started.

It rose beautifully and after ascending about 75 feet, Mike circled around us. We could see Edith waving her handkerchief. I was surprised at her composure. After making one circle, Mike started off, like a huge bird, for Portrush. We watched the airship until it became a speck in the distance. Mr. and Mrs. O'Neill walked back with me to the hotel and I had to earnestly assure Edith's mother that her daughter was in safe hands.

Just before noon I heard a shout, "They're coming back."

I rushed out of the hotel and saw the aeroplane about a half a mile off, bearing down on us with all speed. When they came nearer I saw them rise, and I knew Mike was going to circle. He went up to a height of fully 400 feet, and circled around over the hotel three times. In making the third circle, he went out far over the sea.

The descent was made without difficulty, and the aeroplane touched the ground without a perceptible jar.

Edith jumped out before Mike could descend to help her, and before I reached the aeroplane. She ran at once to her mother and kissed her.

"Edith, child," said her mother, with tears in her eyes, "you must not go flying again."

"Oh, Mamma," said the happy girl, "it was grand. I never, never enjoyed anything like it."

"You rascal," said Mr. O'Neill, smiling, to Mike, "I thought you promised to keep off the sea."

"I made him do it," said Edith, hastily. "He didn't want to, but I wanted to fly above the water."

Mike hung his head. Mike was always proud of keeping his word. It was the atmosphere again. It changed Mike.

Edith cheered him by going to him with outstretched hand, and saying in her sweet, musical voice: "Thank you ever so much, Mr. Connor."

Mike's face brightened and he took off his cap gallantly, saying: "The pleasure was mine, Miss O'Neill."

DUNLUCE CASTLE.

DUNLUCE CASTLE.

After Edith and her parents were gone I asked Mike about the flight.

"Capital, Jack, capital," Mike said with enthusiasm, "I tell you Jack, there are few girls like Edith."

I noticed that he had unconsciously used her first name.

He then gave me some details of the flight. On the return trip, they had paused to circle around Dunluce Castle, and then they had followed the electric railway to the Causeway. This electric railway from Portrush to the Causeway was the first electric railroad that was successfully operated in the world. It was built in 1883, being designed by Sir William Siemens. Formerly it was operated with the third rail, but now it is an overhead trolley. As they were flying along this railroad, about 40 feet high, they overtook a crowded car. When the astonished passengers saw them fly past, their enthusiasm knew no bounds. Edith enjoyed the greeting and waved her handkerchief in return.

Mike wanted to remain a few days longer at the Causeway, but when I told him that Mr. O'Neill had told me he was called back to Dublin the next day, and that his family would accompany him, he decided to start the next day himself.

As we bade the O'Neills goodbye, they gave us a cordial invitation to call on them in Dublin. I was delighted with the invitation, and so was Mike, but for a different reason. I was glad because I knew Mr. O'Neill would show us the places of historic interest in Ireland's capital city, and I was anxious to see a real Irish home. Mike confided to me that he had already arranged to take Miss Edith for a flight over Dublin.

Immediately after breakfast we started. A big crowd cheered us as the aeroplane rose. As we circled around over the crowd, I could see Miss Edith's handkerchief waving us a farewell.

We sailed along the coast from the Causeway towards Ballycastle, 13 miles away. It was as fine a coast as I have ever seen, excepting along County Clare. We passed over several old ruins, and saw the famous Carrick-a-Rede Bridge. Carrick-a-Rede, which means the Rock in the Track, is a gigantic rock, separated from the mainland by a deep channel, sixty feet wide. Fishermen use the rock from March to October, and a bridge has been constructed of cables between the rock and the mainland. This swinging bridge is fully 80 feet above the water. As you cross it, the bridge bends and sways, but the natives cross it continually, often carrying heavy burdens.

We flew over Ballycastle, a clean-looking little fishing village, making great excitement amongst the villagers. It was nine o'clock when we sailed over the town. There is coal in this vicinity, but it has been properly worked.

In the distance we could see Fair Head towering over the Sea. Near Fair Head is Torr Head, which is only twelve and a half miles from the coast of Scotland. This is the shortest distance between the two countries. We could see the Mull of Cantyre very clearly.

After passing Ballycastle, we flew over a surprisingly beautiful region around Cushendal. Mike was now taking more interest in the Irish scenery and I remarked that he had just begun to appreciate the beauty of Ireland. We found Glen Ariff bathed in sunshine, its innumerable waterfalls glistening in the light of the sunbeams. This is a place of rare beauty. As we passed Larne we could see the excited inhabitants climbing on the walls and roofs to get a better view of the monster bird, as our airship looked to be from land.

Larne has a good harbor protected by a curious, curving headland. Mail steamers leave here for Stranraer across the channel, thirty-nine miles. The crossing is made in two hours. This is the shortest crossing between Ireland and Scotland. There is talk of running an underground railway over to Scotland from somewhere near here.

It was at Larne that Edward Bruce, a brother of the famed Robert Bruce of Scotland, landed in 1315, in an ill-fated expedition which he made to Ireland.

A little later we came to Carrickfergus, where Andrew Jackson's father used to live. It is ten miles from Belfast, and in former years was a place of greater importance than its neighbor.

There is an old castle at Carrickfergus, built in 1178, which still defies the ravages of time. It is built on a huge rock, projecting thirty feet out of Belfast Lough, and is a splendid example of a Norman fortress. There are walls in the ruins ninety feet high and nine feet thick.

William III. landed at Carrickfergus in 1690, on his way to the Battle of the Boyne.

We could now see the smoke of Belfast, the Chicago of Ireland. Overlooking it is Cave Hill, a lofty mound, back of the city. As we swept over this great metropolis, we rose to a height of 400 feet, so as to get the best possible view of the busy hive of industry. Tall chimneys sent out smoke. Huge shipyards covered acres and acres, houses extended almost as far as the eye could reach. Church spires pierced the sky in every direction.

As I looked down on Belfast that summer morning, it looked like a model city. Its magnificent business streets, and noble city hall, are in keeping with its fame and enterprise.

Passing directly over it, Mike brought the aeroplane to the ground on a level place near the foot of Cave Hill.

CHAPTER XII

OVER AND AROUND BELFAST

IT was almost 11:00 o'clock when we alit at the foot of Cave Hill. Leaving our airship in charge of an astonished Irishman, whose house was near by, we took a street car down town, and had lunch at the Y. M. C. A. cafe.

Evidently our flight over the city had been observed by many, as we heard a good deal of conversation about the "airship."

We came back to Cave Hill about noon, and I found a great crowd around the aeroplane. Getting a starting rail, Mike prepared to ascend as quickly as possible. Just as we were about ready to start, I saw a young man edge his way through the crowd, with a note book in one hand and a pencil in the other. I recognized him at once as a reporter, seeking an interview. Before he came close enough to hear, I said to Mike: "Hurry up, hurry up. I see a newspaper man."

If I had told Mike I had seen his Satanic Majesty, he could not have hurried his final preparations more, as he has a horror of the "interviewer," and we were determined to escape them while in Ireland.

When the reporter reached my side, he began at once: "I represent the Whig, the Belfast Whig. We want an account of this airship, if you please. What are your names? Where did you come from?" Before he could ask any more questions, Mike shouted loudly to me: "All aboard."

I was glad to leap into my seat. Without another word, Mike vaulted into his place, started the motor, and before the astonished reporter could get out another word, we were sailing in the air.

The big crowd cheered and clapped their hands, as we rose gracefully towards Cave Hill. Ascending to the very summit of this hill, Mike turned the aeroplane in one of his familiar circles, and we made another wide sweep over Belfast. Below us we could see Belfast Castle. The Earl of Shaftesbury, grandson of the famous philanthropist, lives in this Castle, which is a modern mansion, as everything is around Belfast. The Earl has inherited some of the sterling qualities of his illustrious grandfather, and is a public spirited citizen. He was elected Lord Mayor of Belfast in 1907. Belfast is a remarkable city, different from any other city in Ireland. It practically came on the map in the 17th century, when it first became a centre for the export of linen in a small way.

As it is located at the junction of Down and Antrim two Presbyterian Counties, Belfast has always been a Presbyterian stronghold. There are upwards of 60 prosperous Presbyterian churches in the city today, and the Presbyterian Assembly Hall is one of the largest and most beautiful buildings in the North of Ireland.

One hundred years ago Belfast had a population of less than 20,000. Today it has nearly 400,000. Its wealth has doubled six times in the last 25 years.

Belfast owes its prosperity to the linen trade. This industry alone now amounts to sixty million dollars a year. The largest mill, which I could easily distinguish, covers five acres, with 6000 spindles, 1000 looms and more than 4000 employees.

There are also extensive machine shops, and its ship yards build the largest ocean liners afloat.

Here also are manufactured agricultural implements, "soft drinks" of all kinds, and machinery of every sort.

Its situation on Belfast Lough, at the mouth of the Lagan is picturesque, and, taken altogether, Belfast is one of the finest cities in Europe. Leaving it behind us we sailed due south, in the direction of Downpatrick, where St. Patrick is buried.

As we crossed County Down, we admired again the thrifty farm-houses, well-tilled farms, and the little fields, green with potatoes and turnips, or waving with flax and oats.

In less than half an hour Downpatrick came in sight. We flew over the beautiful Gothic Down Cathedral, in the churchyard of which St. Patrick lies buried. Here also lies buried St. Bridget and St. Columba, two other noble characters in Ireland's religious history.

St. Patrick was born in Scotland about the year 387. When he was sixteen years old, he was taken a captive, and sold as a slave to an Irishman, for whom he herded sheep and swine in County Antrim.

While a slave, he became a devout Christian, and made his escape when he was twenty-two years old. He entered a monastic school in France, and fitted himself as a Missionary to Ireland. At that time the Irish worshipped at Druid altars.

Landing at the mouth of the Slaney in County Down, he settled in Downpatrick. He remained here several years and then visited all parts of the island, meeting with marvelous success. In 457 he settled in Armagh and lived there for eight years.

While visiting in Downpatrick in his 78th year, he was seized with a fatal illness, and died at the scene of early labors. Here he was buried.

St. Bridget was born near Armagh about 453. She was rich and beautiful, but became a convert to Christianity, and devoted her life to missionary labors amongst the Irish. She died in 525, and was first buried at Kildare. Her remains and those of St. Columba were brought to Downpatrick in 1185. St. Patrick made the shamrock the national flower of Ireland by teaching from its three petals the doctrine of the Trinity.

Turning west from Downpatrick, Mike and I followed in the air St. Patrick's footsteps to Armagh. Before entering County Armagh, we crossed over a pretty village, called Banbridge. County Armagh resembles County Down in its general appearance. It was a beautiful picture of rural quietude. It was after two o'clock when we caught our first glimpse of the famous Irish city of Armagh.

This is Ireland's most sacred city. Two Primates of Ireland live here, and here are two Archbishops, and two magnificent Cathedrals. Armagh is a well-built town of some 8,000 inhabitants. It is built partly on a hill, which makes some of its streets quite steep. A Cathedral was founded here by St. Patrick in 432. His Eminence, Cardinal Logue, an able and learned divine, is the Roman Catholic Primate, while Dr. Alexander is the Protestant Primate of the island. The ecclesiastical head of the Presbyterian Church is called the Moderator, and is elected every year.

We sailed over the beautiful grounds of Dr. Alexander's Palace, and were reminded of his gifted wife, who wrote:

"There is a green hill far away,

Outside a city wall

Where the dear Lord was crucified,

Who died to save us all."

Mrs. Alexander died in 1895. Another well known poem of hers is "The Burial of Moses."

There are three prosperous and growing Presbyterian churches in Armagh. Dr. John Hall, who afterwards became one of the foremost preachers in America, was pastor of one of these Presbyterian churches for a time, and laid the foundation of his future fame in this city. There is a vigorous Methodist church, which is also active in promoting the Christian faith.

Armagh is rich in historic memories. As I circled over its steep and winding streets that day with Mike, I thought of all the scenes enacted on the soil beneath.

Here St. Patrick lived. Here a great educational institution flourished more than 1200 years ago. As many as 7000 students gathered in this place at one time to attend its far-famed University.

The bleeding body of Brian Boru was reverently carried here, after the fatal day at Clontarf in 1014. In the stirring years of the O'Neills, Armagh saw many exciting scenes. But all was quiet and peaceful on that lovely summer day, as we circled over the sacred city, and flew south toward Newry.

CHAPTER XIII

ALIGHTING IN DROGHEDA

ON our way from Armagh to Newry, we saw the Newry Canal. This little piece of engineering work was completed shortly before the railroads came to make it useless.

Newry is a prosperous place, but not noted much in history. The Newryites gazed at us in wonder, as we whirled directly over their town towards Warrenpoint. Warrenpoint is a handsome seaside resort at the head of Carlingford Bay. We kept to the east side of the Bay until we reached Rosstrevor. This beautiful village has a back-ground of wooded hills, and many handsome villas are in its neighborhood. The village is owned by Sir John Ross-of-Blandensburg. A large obelisk in an elevated place tells why the name of the owner is "Ross of Blandensburg." This obelisk is in honor of General Ross, grandfather of Sir John, and the inscription reads as follows:

The Officers of a Grateful Army
Which under the command of the lamented Major General Robert Ross
Attacked and defeated the American forces at Blandensburg
on the 24th of August, 1814 and on the same day
Victoriously entered Washington, the Capital of the United States
Inscribe upon this tablet their admiration of his professional skill and their
esteem for his amiable private character.

As I pointed out the obelisk to Mike and told him of this inscription, he was greatly amused.

From Rosstrevor we crossed the little bay to Carlingford, another picturesque village, and shortly afterwards sighted Dundalk.

"What time is it?" asked Mike.

I looked at my watch and answered:

"Ten minutes to three."

"Let us alight here," said Mike. "My wings are tired."

We came down in a field just outside of the town. It was the worst landing Mike made. We alit on one runner of the aeroplane, and got a severe jar, but, fortunately, no damage was done.

After an hour's rest and a walk around town, we sailed on to Drogheda, where we expected to spend the night.

If we had been Theodore Roosevelt himself, or even Edward VII., we could not have attracted more attention and honor from the people of the country than we did that afternoon between Dundalk and Drogheda. Mike made a superb landing at Drogheda. We alit beside a two-storied house on the edge of town, creating a sensation. Some children, near the door, saw us swooping down, and ran, screaming into the house. Just as we were landing a woman ran out and as she saw the aeroplane alight, she uttered a shriek, as though she had seen a ghost.

Presently a man came running, and we introduced ourselves. Leaving the aeroplane with him and the gathering crowd, we went to a hotel. I was interested in Drogheda, on account of its historic siege by Oliver Cromwell in 1649. We saw two of the old towers standing, just as they were left after the siege.

Oliver Cromwell is as unpopular in Ireland as the Duke of Alva in the Netherlands, and when we read his report of his doings at this city we were not surprised. Here is what he wrote from Drogheda in reporting to Parliament:

"Divers of the enemy retreated to the Milmount, a place very strong and of difficult access, being exceedingly high, having a good graft, and strongly palisadoed. The Governor, Sir Arthur Aston, and divers considerable officers being there, our men getting up to them, were ordered by me to put them all to the sword. And, indeed, being in the heat of action, I forbade them to spare any that were in arms in the town; and I think that night they put to the sword about 2000 men. Then our horse and foot followed them so fast over the bridge, which goes over a broad river; and being very long and houses on both sides, yet they had not time to pull up their draw bridge, that our men fell violently upon them, and I believe there were 2000 of them put to the sword. Divers of the officers and soldiers being fled over the bridge into the other parts of the town, where about 100 of them possessed St. Peters church-steeple, some the West Gate, others a strong round tower next the gate called St. Sundays. These being summoned to yield to mercy refused, whereupon I ordered the steeple of St. Peters to be fired, when one of them was heard to say in the midst of the flames, 'God confound me, I burn! I burn!'

"The next day the two other towers were summoned, in one of which was about six or seven score, but they refused to yield themselves; and we, knowing that hunger must compel them, set only good guards to secure them from running away until their stomachs were come down. From one of the said towers, notwithstanding their condition, they killed and wounded some of our men. When they submitted, their officers WERE KNOCKED ON

THE HEAD, and every tenth man of the soldiers killed, and the rest shipped for the Barbadoes."

After writing this gentle epistle, Oliver continues:

"I am persuaded that this is a righteous judgment of God upon these barbarous wretches, who have embrued their hands in so much innocent blood, and that it will tend to prevent the effusion of blood, for the future, which are the satisfactory grounds for such actions, which otherwise cannot but work remorse and regret."

After viewing Drogheda, we hired a jaunting car, and visited the ruins of Monasterboice, some six miles from town. This monastery was founded by St. Patrick. Eight or nine centuries ago, thousands of students gathered here every year. There are two small churches left still standing, evidently of great age. Our driver told us that the big round tower there was 1000 years old. The finest relics of the past here are three large Celtic Crosses, the largest being 27 feet in height. One of them is badly damaged, and, of course, the damage is attributed to Cromwell.

Our driver was a talkative fellow and entertained us with all kinds of stories about the country.

IRISH JAUNTING CAR.

"I always tell folks," he said to Mike, "all that I know, but begorra, I keep the rest to myself."

He got a good laugh on Mike when he told us some history which Mike deemed ridiculous.

"Do you think I'm a fool to tell me that," said Mike.

"Sure, I don't know, sor," answered the driver solemnly, "I only met you this evening."

This driver had a son in America, as a good many Irish fathers have. These Irish boys go out to America with very little that they own except their names, but they soon begin to make remittances home, and in thousands of Irish homes the regular remittances from faithful sons and daughters in America are depended on as part of the means of livelihood.

The river which Cromwell refers to in his dispatches, on which Drogheda is built, is the Boyne river. Three miles from Drogheda, on the banks of the Boyne, the armies of William III. and James II. met in battle. This was the battle that sealed the fate of King James, and it is said he showed a little too much anxiety for his royal person on this occasion to win much renown as a soldier. The battle was fought on July 12th, 1690. A huge obelisk now marks the field of conflict.

The Boyne is a beautiful stream, richly wooded, with many villas adorning its banks. This part of Ireland is "soggy," as Mike expressed it, with historic memories. The next day we hoped to fly over Tara, the ancient Capital of the Green Isle, and with pleasant anticipation, we retired for the night.

CHAPTER XIV

WITH FRIENDS IN DUBLIN

EARLY next morning we ascended from Drogheda, and followed the valley of the Boyne for several miles. Then turning south, we flew over County Meath, on a straight way to Tara, the ancient Capital of Ireland.

County Meath is one of the most fertile spots in Europe. Its rich greenness is proverbial. Large pasturages, though not profitable to the peasants, add to the beauty of the landscape.

"I say, Jack," said Mike, after we had been gazing in silence at the fields as they glided under us, "I am falling in love with Ireland."

"Mike," I said solemnly, "you mean that you are falling in love with the Irish. I think it is because we are getting near Dublin you are feeling that way."

"We'll get to Dublin bright and early at this rate," said Mike evasively. I fancied I could see Mike become more and more lively as we approached the neighborhood of Dublin.

As we saw Tara with its little cluster of Irish cottages, I felt a sense of disappointment, but when we circled over the famous hill, I let my imagination supply what was wanting. I re-peopled the green mounds with Druid priests and Irish Kings. I imagined coronation scenes, and vast armies filling the plains. These used to be realities in Tara, but all is changed now. An air of loneliness pervades the very atmosphere. Even the "Stone of Destiny," fabled as Jacob's Pillow at Bethel, is gone. It was carried to Scotland centuries ago, and later taken to London, where it can be seen as the seat of the coronation chair in Westminster Abbey. We saw the Statue of St. Patrick, at which many a rude joke is made. From our aerial viewpoint we could not see it distinctly, but it is said to be a fair work of art for a stone cutter to accomplish. St. Patrick often preached at Tara, and a shaft here in his honor would be most appropriate.

Daniel O'Connell on one occasion drew a quarter of a million of people to Tara in 1844, when he held a great two days' political meeting and gave two brilliant addresses.

Tara is not marked by any marble obelisk to recount its former glories, but it will be held in memory while time lasts on account of Thomas Moore's world-famed ballad:

"The Harp that once through Tara's Halls

The soul of music shed

Now hangs as mute on Tara's walls,

As if that soul were fled.

So sleeps the pride of former days,

So glory's thrill is o'er,

So hearts that once beat high for praise

Now feel that pulse no more.

"No more to chiefs and ladies bright

The harp of Tara swells;

The chord alone that breaks at night

Its tale of ruin tells.

Thus Freedom now so seldom wakes,

The only throb she gives

Is when some heart indignant breaks

To show that she still lives."

"Farewell to Tara's Halls," I said, as we swept on south.

As we fled over Ireland we astonished the Irish people, but we also astonished the denizens of the air. The birds seemed unable to understand what kind of a monster was invading their element. As we passed over rookeries, where the crows had their nests in large flocks, the cawing of the frightened crows was tremendous. The little sparrows chirped around us with their chatter. We saw many magpies, robins, blackbirds and thrushes. There was one bird in Ireland I learned to love, the meadow lark. It would spring from the ground singing as it rose, until it was lost in the clouds, but its sweet notes could still be heard.

Less than half an hour after leaving Tara, we arrived at Maynooth, which is located just 12 miles west of Dublin. Maynooth is celebrated as the seat of Maynooth College, the chief Roman Catholic educational center in modern Ireland. A College was established in Maynooth as early as 1513, but the present institution dates back only to 1795. At that time it was re-organized and established with Government grants.

Three-fourths of the priests in Ireland have been educated here, and the standard of the college is high amongst the Catholic institutions of Europe. About 150 complete their education every year, and take their place as the spiritual leaders of the Catholic population of the Island. Until the establishment of Maynooth College, the Irish priests were educated generally in France. Maynooth is noted amongst all classes in Ireland as a center for temperance reform, and it is claimed that fully three-fourths of the priests from Maynooth are pledged abstainers, and ardent temperance workers. The College has a large, spacious campus, and adequate buildings, and has an attendance of about 500 students.

The massive ruins of Maynooth Castle stand at the gateway of the College. There is another interesting ruin in the vicinity, the Round Tower, of Taghadoc, one of the largest of these Irish Round Towers. It stands a few miles south of Maynooth.

We circled twice over the College, and were greeted with cheers by a company of the students who were walking on the campus.

"Now for Dublin," said Mike, as he turned the aeroplane east.

"Mike," I said, "do you know why every Irishman ought to be rich?"

"No," he answered, "I never knew that was one of the duties of an Irishman."

"Yes," I went on, "every Irishman ought to be rich because the capital of the country has been "dublin" every year for centuries."

"That's a *capital* joke," said Mike laughing.

As we were leaving Maynooth, I could see from my lofty seat the famous Carton House. In this lordly mansion lives one of the most favored of Irishmen, the Duke of Leinster. He has a whole bushel of titles, is worth millions of money and has the blood of a hundred Dukes and Earls in his veins. In spite of all this, he is not very robust in physical health, and it is said he has symptoms of tuberculosis. He is young and unmarried. He has several palatial residences, but Carton House is his favorite. It stands in a Park, enclosed by an eight mile 10 foot wall, and in the Park are over thirty miles of macadamized driveways. His garden covers sixty acres. Queen Victoria was once the guest of this splendid home, which is a royal palace itself.

For a number of miles we followed the river Liffey, and it was easy to tell we were nearing the Capital City. Beautiful villas dotted the landscape, and many of these homes were evidently abodes of wealth and culture.

As we came nearer, we rose in the air until we were fully 600 feet high. From this lofty elevation I could see the great city of Dublin, stretching to the sea, and reaching out on both sides along Dublin Bay. Mr. O'Neill had described his home to us so clearly that we had no difficulty in finding it. He lived south of Dublin, near Blackrock, not far from the seaside.

We followed the river Liffey as we passed through the center of the city. To our left we saw Phoenix Park on the western outskirts. We passed Four Courts, a massive Government building. We could see the famed Dublin Castle, south of the river, and further on Trinity College with its large campus in the middle of the city.

Passing over Trinity College Park, we began to scan the landscape for Mr. O'Neill's residence. We could see that we attracted great attention from the populace and we saw thousands of upturned faces of astonished Dublinmen. Mike's quick eye discerned our landing place. The home of "The" O'Neill, as we heard him called in Dublin, was in the center of a large park, with a tall wall circling it completely. In front of the noble mansion there was a large lawn, which made a good place to alight.

It was only nine o'clock when we dismounted from our aeroplane at "Shaneville," as the house was called. Mr. O'Neill and Miss Edith came out of the large front door, as we alit.

"Yankee birds, Yankee birds," sang out the girl in gay greeting.

"Welcome, gentlemen," said Mr. O'Neill, "welcome to 'Shaneville'."

With genuine Irish cordiality he ushered us into his beautiful and richly-furnished home.

CHAPTER XV

GUESTS IN AN IRISH HOME

MIKE and I were glad to rest quietly all that day within the high walls that surrounded "Shaneville." Here we were safe from interviewers, curious people, and an excited populace.

When aeroplaning is as common as motoring now is, it will be much more pleasant. Nowadays an aeroplane makes as much excitement as a comet, and I expect that even this record will read like a novel to some. There are people who might enjoy the notoriety which an aeroplane gives, but we were not anxious to get famous in that way.

During our pleasant day at "Shaneville," I renewed my conversation with Mr. O'Neill in regard to his native land, and, in his library that afternoon we had a long talk again on Ireland.

I noticed that the coat of arms of "Shaneville" was a red hand, with the cross of St. George, and I had remarked that I saw that coat of arms somewhere before. Mr. O'Neill laughed heartily, and assured me he was confident I had seen it often. He told me that was the coat of arms of Ulster, now, and was seen everywhere in the North of Ireland. It was his family which gave Ulster this sign. Long centuries before when his ancestors came over from Scotland to Ireland, the invaders agreed amongst themselves that whoever touched the shore of Ireland first with his hand would be King. An O'Neill amongst them, when the boat stranded on the beach, promptly drew his sharp sword, and cut off his left hand and threw it high on the beach, and was at once hailed as King by the rest. Since that the O'Neill emblem has been a red hand. Mr. O'Neill related how his family held power from that time until the beginning of the 17th century, when a rebellion against England cost them their power and estates in Ulster. It was at this time that Ulster was colonized anew from Scotland.

James I. confiscated nearly all Ulster, and partitioned out the land to new settlers, mostly from Scotland. Although this act had meant the ruin of his house. I could see no bitterness in O'Neill's voice as he spoke of this "plantation of Ulster," as he called it. He said that these new settlers had made good, industrious citizens, and that Ulster was the most prosperous part of Ireland today. He spoke highly of the character of these Scotch-Irishmen, and added:

"You know, sir, away back our own people came from Scotland."

Still, I could see that O'Neill looked on these great real estate transfers by the kings of England as wrongs to the native Irish.

O'Neill told me there were three reforms going on in Ireland in which he had hearty sympathy. These are the improvement of Irish agriculture, the revival of the Gaelic tongue, and the suppression of intemperance amongst the Irish people.

"One splendid result of the agitation for these reforms," he said earnestly, "is that Irishmen are beginning to see that there is one Ireland after all. All creeds in Ireland are united in promoting these great reforms, and it is creating a national sentiment which is bringing all Irishmen into sympathy with each other."

"Our curse has been," he continued, "that we have been divided so much amongst ourselves."

I was surprised when he told me of the Government's present efforts to improve Irish agriculture. There is an Agricultural Department, which furnishes instructors on such subjects as improving of crops, and stock, butter and poultry. They also furnish seeds and fertilizers, and are doing a great deal in promoting prosperity in the backward parts of the island. Mr. O'Neill was enthusiastic about the Gaelic revival.

"Why," he said, "they are even teaching Gaelic now in the National Schools of Ireland. In former times the use of the native tongue was discouraged in every way by the Government, but now teachers are being trained to teach it."

I suggested to him that the English was quite a useful language, since it was spoken in America, and so widely throughout the world.

"We still expect to use English, of course," he exclaimed. He then explained that the efforts of Douglas Hyde and his friends were to make the Irish a bi-lingual people, just as the Welsh are.

In speaking of the progress of this interesting revival of Gaelic in Ireland he gave me some facts.

In 1901 as many as 638,000 could speak Gaelic in Ireland, and the number is constantly increasing. All the churches in Ireland, Protestant, and Catholic, have endorsed the movement. There is a strong Gaelic League, which employs over a dozen lecturers and organizers, who promote the study of Gaelic all over the island. I was assured that even in America there was a strong branch of this Gaelic League, and Mr. O'Neill told me that Mr. Roosevelt had endorsed the work highly.

O'Neill was also deeply interested in the temperance reform.

"Ireland," he said to me, "has been a place where they have had too much good whisky and too much bad politics. These two things have ruined us."

He spoke with much pride of the fact that scientific temperance instruction had been introduced into the National schools of Erin in 1905, and also told of the work that all the churches were doing. He was an ardent admirer of Father Mathew.

"A real temperance apostle," he exclaimed, "one of God's best blessings to Ireland since the days of St. Patrick."

He spoke cordially of the temperance leaders, and told me of the good work being done at Maynooth college by the Faculty and the students. He said that America's eminent churchman, Archbishop Ireland, had helped the temperance cause in Ireland, which is his native land. He also mentioned Rev. John Macmillan, of Belfast, the temperance leader among the Presbyterians in Ireland, and said he was a noble temperance patriot.

"These reforms," he repeated, "are bringing us together and giving a feeling of unity to Irishmen such as they have not had since the days of Brian Boru."

I asked him what he thought of Ireland's relation to England.

He paused a few moments before answering, and when he did reply it was in a low, quiet tone.

"We must forget the past," he said, "if Ireland is to make progress. It is true that England has cruelly wronged Ireland. My own family has suffered in past generations, suffered shamefully. But the English Government of today is treating Ireland very differently. Gladstone inaugurated a new era, through the efforts of Parnell, Redmond, and our modern Irish leaders. Today the English people, I believe, want Ireland to have justice."

I asked him what he thought of separation from England. He answered at once: "We cannot be separated. God has placed the islands side by side. What we want is freedom to manage internal affairs, just as the States in America, just as Canada, Australia, and New Zealand. We want local-self government, but we must remain a part of the British Empire."

He went on to tell me how the Irishmen had helped to build up the British Empire, and make it what it is today.

"The present ambassador of the British Empire in Washington," he exclaimed, "is an Irishman."

I was profoundly impressed with his views on this subject. I could see he was a man with wide sympathy and practical outlook, and believed in living for the future, rather than the past. He still had all the fire of the O'Neill blood in his veins, but it had been disciplined by generations of suffering.

We had a happy time in the evening. There is no hospitality like the Irish hospitality. It is whole-hearted, cordial and sincere.

Miss Edith delighted us with several Irish songs. She sang Moore's touching melody: "The Last Rose of Summer," with genuine pathos. Afterwards she began on American songs, and when she had sung several, I remarked that she sang like an American.

She turned around on her piano stool and replied: "I have always admired America. Sometimes I tell my father that I believe that I was meant for an American woman."

"Cross the ocean, Miss O'Neill," said Mike quickly, "and a thousand Americans will swear that you were meant for an American man."

Edith blushed and turned again to the piano.

"Tut, tut," said Mr. O'Neill to Mike, "you have been kissing the Blarney Stone since you came to Ireland."

"It's the atmosphere," I remarked, "Mr. Connor gets more like an Irishman every day."

"Did you ever hear what the citizens of Dublin did when the Union of 1801 was agitated?" asked Mr. O'Neill. "They held an indignation meeting, and resolved to burn everything that was imported from England, except *coal*." As we laughed heartily at this, Mr. O'Neill went on: "Our coachman made a curious remark to me today about you gentlemen and your aeroplane. He said you ought to feel proud of this trip you are making over Ireland in the air, for you are going *where the foot of man never trod before*."

"This coachman amused me shortly after I first hired him. There is a bad hole back of the stable, and I forgot to say anything to him about it until I found he had fallen into it, and hurt himself severely. I told him I was sorry I had forgotten to tell him about it."

"That's all right, Master," he replied, "I found it myself."

CHAPTER XVI

AROUND THE CAPITAL CITY OF IRELAND

THE next morning after breakfast, Mr. O'Neill drove his motor car in front of the house, and Miss O'Neill, Mike and I joined him for a day around Dublin.

I took my seat beside Mr. O'Neill, and Mike and Edith sat together in the rear.

We had a delightful day, and the memory of that trip around this interesting city will always be one of my happiest memories.

Our first visit was Trinity College, with its campus of 47 acres in the heart of Dublin. The main building, at the entrance, is a noble structure. We entered Examination Hall, where many an Irish brain has been violently cudgelled at examination time. There is a fine portrait hung on its walls of Queen Elizabeth, who founded Trinity. The chapel is a modest building. The Library is famed as containing Brian Boru's harp. It is said that this harp suggested to Moore his ode on Tara. Here we also saw the "Book of Kells", so called because it came from the Monastery at Kells.

In this book the four gospels are written out with exquisite penmanship, on leaves embossed with gold, and beautifully illuminated. We doubt if there is a more beautiful book in the world.

Coming out of Trinity, Mr. O'Neill called our attention to the statues of Edmund Burke and Oliver Goldsmith, which adorn the entrance. These are two of the most famous of Trinity's sons.

Opposite the entrance to Trinity is the old Parliament House, in which in former days the Irish Parliament met. It is now used by the bank of Ireland. It was in this building that Grattan thundered his anathemas against the foes of Ireland.

Dublin is a city of monuments. As Mr. O'Neill showed them to us, we began to have a better appreciation of the number of eminent men whom Ireland has given to the world.

High above them all, in the centre of the city, is a lofty pillar, 134 feet high, erected to the honor of the great English Admiral, Lord Nelson. From the base of Nelson's monument street cars start in all directions.

Daniel O'Connell's monument is a fitting tribute to Ireland's great Liberator. It is 12 feet high and is surrounded by a number of smaller figures. There are also statues of the two great Irish Statesmen, remarkable for their patriotic eloquence, Henry Grattan, and John Philpot Curran.

Mr. O'Neill also pointed out the statue to Father Mathew, which stands in a central place. It is a noble work of art, done in marble, and is worthy of the Apostle of Temperance. Thomas Moore, the gifted poet, has been honored by his countrymen also, although his poems will keep his memory green as long as time lasts.

A statue to Charles Stewart Parnell is to be erected Mr. O'Neill told us. O'Neill has been a great admirer of Parnell, and the tragic close of his life grieved him much.

We had a delightful time in Phoenix Park. This unrivalled combination of forest and meadow, flowerbeds and fountains, driveways and lawns, covers 1700 acres, and is a credit to Ireland.

There is a statue of the Duke of Wellington, Ireland's foremost soldier, in Phoenix Park. It is like Washington's Monument in Washington, except that it is only one-third as large.

We visited the zoological gardens in the Park. Here we saw a marvelous collection of all kinds of animals.

As we went through the Monkey house, Mike said to Edith: "In America some wise men think we sprang from monkeys."

"The Irish didn't," she said gaily, "we never *sprang from anybody*. We sprang at them."

As we laughed at her wit, Mike remarked:

"I have always objected to having a monkey tied on to my family tree."

Mr. O'Neill took us to the Viceregal lodge, which is in Phoenix Park, where the Lord Lieutenant of Ireland lives in the summer time, and we had a brief audience with His Excellency. He professed to be much pleased to see us, and was greatly interested in our aerial exploits in the Irish atmosphere.

We also visited Dublin Castle, the center of Irish history for centuries. We saw there the tower in which Robert Emmet and Lord Edward Fitzgerald were confined, over a century ago, after their ill-fated rebellions. Oliver Cromwell resided in this castle for a time. William III. visited it in 1690. The

Castle is at present the scene of many gay social events during the winter months, when the Lord Lieutenant resides in it.

Stephen's Green is an aristocratic suburb of twenty-two acres in the heart of Dublin. It is a big square, surrounded by the mansions of the rich and titled of Dublin's citizenship.

We motored also a little to the south of Dublin and visited Clontarf, where the famous battle was fought on Good Friday in 1014 between the Irish and the Danes. In this battle Brian Boru was killed. Brian marched his army that day from Phoenix Park, where he was encamped, and defeated the Danes, but one of the fleeing Danish generals slew the aged Brian.

There are two famed Cathedrals in Dublin. St. Patrick's Cathedral, where Dean Swift formerly preached, is a fine cruciform church, in the early pointed style. In it there are monuments to both the Dean and "Stella" his wife. This Cathedral was founded in 1190 but had varied experiences in history. It was "restored" in 1865, at a cost of over $800,000, by Sir Benjamin Guinness.

The Roman Catholic Pro-Cathedral is in Marlborough Street, and is built in Doric style. The magnificent altar is of white marble. The music in the services is especially fine.

We planned to leave Dublin the first of the next week and continue our way southward. We spent a quiet Sunday at "Shaneville" attending divine services with the O'Neills.

The next morning Edith obtained permission from her father and mother to take her much anticipated flight over Dublin. The ascent was made at ten o'clock. Edith was dressed in a neat-fitting white dress, with white gloves and veil to match, when she appeared on the lawn, ready to start. She looked so charming as she seated herself in the aeroplane, that I could not help exclaiming.

"These Irish birds are rare creatures."

"Watch the Irish dove and the American Eagle soar," said Mike, as he started the motor. We waved goodbye as the aeroplane rose in the air, and disappeared over the trees.

While they were gone Mr. O'Neill took me for a final stroll over his pleasant grounds.

"I have never visited America," he told me, "but I am anxious to cross the Atlantic, and see your marvelous country. America holds the future." He expressed high admiration for the leaders in America, especially President Roosevelt and William Jennings Bryan.

"I met Mr. Bryan a few years ago here in Dublin," he said. "We were all delighted with him. He is a great and good man. He told me there was Irish blood in his veins and he was proud of it." Mr. O'Neill also expressed the highest admiration for Abraham Lincoln, and called him a benefactor to all the world.

I cordially invited him to visit the land of the Stars and Stripes.

In half an hour Edith and Mike returned. Mike circled over the house, in his usual way before alighting and then made a good landing just where he had started from.

With her face flushed and happy, Edith stepped lightly to the grass.

"Papa, papa," she cried, as Mr. O'Neill came forward to greet her, "You must get an aeroplane."

"My child," said her fond parent, "I am afraid this old bird has walked too long to learn to fly now."

"What did you see?" I asked.

"O, everything," she answered, "it was grand. We went away out as far as the Golf Grounds at Malahide, and all over Phoenix Park. Won't you come back again Mr. Connor," she said, turning to Mike who was standing beside his airship.

Mike took off his cap and bowed.

"I surely will," he said so emphatically, that the color came to Edith's cheeks.

As I looked at them, already such cordial friends, and realized that they had never met until a few days before, I said to myself:

"It's the Irish atmosphere."

CHAPTER XVII

WICKLOW, THE GARDEN OF IRELAND

AFTER dinner that day we bade our friends farewell. Mr. and Mrs. O'Neill were urgent in their invitation that we visit them again.

"Good-bye," said Edith to Mike. "I am very glad I have met you, and I thank you for the pleasure of flying with you."

"Do not mention it," said Mike as he held her hand, "You are such a brave aeronaut that I could fly with you anywhere."

Edith blushed deeply as Mike's eyes spoke as well as his tongue.

After we had ascended in the air, Mike circled around, like a carrier pigeon, and then sped off toward the south.

As we entered County Wicklow, we left the seacoast and crossed Wicklow about the middle of the County, passing over the Wicklow hills.

This was the most exciting part of our entire trip.

Wicklow has been called a miniature Switzerland, and it well deserves the name. There are over twenty mountains in this small space that exceed 2000 feet in height, and as they rise abruptly from the level, they seem even higher.

Scattered among these hills, there are beautiful valleys, magnificent mansions, villas, farms and Irish cottages. Much of the country is thickly wooded. The Woods of Shillelah are in Wicklow. Here the best blackthorn, out of which Ireland's ancient weapon was made, used to grow, and the weapons were called "Shillelahs" from these woods.

In order to see the grandeur of Wicklow to the best advantage, Mike and I threw discretion to the winds. The motor had been acting so well since we left County Derry, that we had full confidence in it now.

"Let us go over the tops of the mountains," I said to Mike.

He was glad to do this, and rose until we reached the dizzy height of 2500 feet. I would not advise aeroplanists to seek this altitude until they are thoroughly acclimated to life in the atmosphere.

I had become somewhat hardened to aeroplaning, but as I looked straight down sometimes into a deep valley, half a mile below me, I did not feel altogether at my ease.

The view was magnificent. We passed over the Valley of Glendalough, between the mountains of Coomaderry and Lugduff. In this dark valley, by the side of a lake, St. Kevin lived in an early day. His fear of womankind has been immortalized by Moore. Formerly in this valley there was a crowded city, and a great seat of learning, and many kings are buried in this vicinity.

We saw here the ruins of the Seven Churches, and a Round Tower, said to date back to the 7th century.

As we entered the vale of Avoca, I remarked to Mike that Thomas Moore had touched Ireland with his genius, just as Sir Walter Scott threw a charm over Scotland. The vale of Avoca is best known by Moore's lines:

"Sweet Vale of Avoca, how calm could I rest,

In thy bosom of shade, with friends I love best;

Where the storms that we feel in this cold world should cease,

And our hearts, like thy waters, be mingled in peace."

Although the scenery through Wicklow was grand, I felt relieved as we quitted our lofty altitude, and sailed nearer the earth over the more prosaic County of Wexford. As Mike lowered the aeroplane within about 100 feet of the land I breathed easier.

Wexford was the home of Dermot McMurragh, who first invited the English into Ireland. The ruins of his castle and his tomb are near Ferns, but Wexford is not particularly proud of McMurragh.

Wexford has been called by an Irishman, "the most agricultural county in Ireland," and we could well believe it as we swept over its green pastures and cultivated farms.

We sighted the city of Wexford at 4:00 o'clock. As we circled around over the city, I observed its excellent harbor, with a complete breakwater, and also its spacious docks. The city looks like a city in Palestine on account of its narrow streets, but it is a clean, prosperous looking place.

We alit, as usual outside the city, and left our aeroplane for the night in charge of a friendly farmer. We made our escape as quietly as possible from the gathering crowd, and soon found the quiet of a good hotel. The Redmond family, noted Irish leaders, reside in Wexford, and the spirit of the dislike to England is very pronounced.

We saw two magnificent churches called the Twins, on account of their similarity. These show the religious zeal of the people. The business part of the town showed their commercial enterprise.

The Quay is a busy place as steamship lines run to England, and there is much traffic in merchandise between Wexford and England, but there is none in affection.

Before retiring for the night we met an interesting old Irishman, whose whole soul was controlled by hatred of Cromwell and England. He had none of Mr. O'Neill's charity for ancient wrongs, and, as he told us of Cromwell's Wexford campaign, we could sympathize with him a good deal. To show us how Ireland regarded Cromwell, he quoted from an Irish poet, a few lines, which ran something like this:

"From Drogheda that man of guilt

To fated Wexford flew,

The red blood reeking on his hilt

Of hearts to Erin true.

He found them there—the young, the old,

The maiden and the wife;

Their guardians brave in death were cold,

Who dared for them in strife.

They prayed for mercy, God on high

Before Thy Cross they prayed,

And ruthless Cromwell bade them die

To glut the Saxon blade."

IRISH VILLAGE

IRISH VILLAGE

After a while we turned the old patriot's attention to America, and we found he had a deep interest in the New World. "It's God's country over there," he told us. We found he had friends in America, and he gave us a ludicrous verse in which some Irishman had described the American character.

"He'd kiss a Queen till he'd raise a blister,

With his arms round her neck, and old felt hat on

And address a King by the name of Mister,

And ask him the price of the throne he sat on."

Mike and I assured him that the Irish poet was too severe on the Yankee.

"Tell us a good Irish story," I said, before we separated.

"I will that," he said, and he told us this one.

An excited orator during the American Civil War, exclaimed:

"We have taken Atlanta: we have taken Savannah, Columbus, Charleston, and now at last, have captured Petersburg, and occupy Richmond: and what remains for us to take?"

An Irishman in the crowd shouted: "Let's take a drink."

As he closed the story our genial friend pointed towards the bar of the hotel in a significant way, and we saw the direction of his joke. We declined politely to show our friendship in this way, but we bade him good-night with a warm handshake and best wishes for the good of Ireland.

CHAPTER XVIII

BACK AGAIN TO CORK

WE left Wexford the next morning in a misty rain.

"I am glad I put a rain-coat on my aeroplane," said Mike as the rain came down in a regular pour.

We did not enjoy that morning's sail from Wexford to Waterford. In an hour's time we saw Waterford arise out of the mist. Like Wexford, Waterford is an important seaport, built on the banks of the Suir river. The name of this beautiful river is a vile slander. Much agricultural produce, and bacon and live stock are shipped from here to England.

The city was able to defend itself against Cromwell in 1649, and was the only place in Ireland that did not fall before the terrible charge of Cromwell's Ironsides.

I was able to see, though indistinctly, the Cathedral, where Strongbow, Ireland's first English master, lies buried. This arch-enemy of Ireland is surely well buried as he has also a tomb in Dublin. Strongbow married the daughter of Dermot McMurragh on the battle field near Waterford where he defeated the Irish.

Lord Roberts has a home in Waterford, and it was here he grew up and developed those fighting qualities which have made him England's foremost soldier today.

Waterford was founded by the Danes in the ninth century. The antique iron bridge across the river, and the docks, a mile long, are notable features of the modern city.

There is one interesting relic of the Danish period still standing near the docks. It is a large round tower, about 50 feet high, which was built by Reginald, the Dane, in 1003. At present it is a police cell.

We left Waterford with the rain still falling, and went up along the banks of the Suir to Portlaw, a small manufacturing town. Near here we flew over Curraghmore, the stately mansion of the Marquis of Waterford. The desmesne covers 5000 acres, and is a beautiful natural park, with many slopes, and dells. There is an ancient castle beside the modern mansion.

In this part of Ireland Sir Walter Raleigh and Edmund Spencer lived. We soon saw Youghal, on the coast, where Raleigh lived, and where his old house still stands.

Edmund Spencer was a close friend of Raleigh's. He was an English poet but became associated with Ireland because he wrote the "Fairy Queen in the Emerald Isle" in 1589 and 1590. He would be more popular in Ireland today only, unfortunately, the Maiden Queen Elizabeth gave him a present of some 3028 acres of Irish land. The Queen's title to this piece of real estate was not considered very good by the Irish, and they have never forgiven Spencer for accepting it.

Sir Walter Raleigh also accepted a big farm of over 40,000 acres in Ireland from this same Maiden Queen, whose real estate transactions in Ireland were considerable, but Raleigh has been partly forgiven because he gave Ireland the potato.

It was nearly nine when we whizzed over Youghal, and circled around it twice. We dipped, as we flew over the harbor, until we were within thirty feet of the water, and aroused excited cheering from the crowd watching us on the docks, as we turned and rose high again over the city.

I discovered Myrtle Lodge, Raleigh's old home in Youghal. It was ivy clad, and well preserved, and the grounds around it neatly kept. I was delighted to see the garden of Myrtle Lodge. It is almost as sacred to the Irishman as the Garden of Eden. In this garden in 1586 Sir Walter Raleigh planted the first potato ever grown in the Emerald Isle. He brought the seed from the West Indies, where they had been carried by the Spanish from Peru, the potato's native home.

It was a century after this before the sterling qualities of the potato were appreciated fully, but now that useful tuber is adopted as Ireland's own darling vegetable.

Sir Walter Raleigh was quite a gardener, as well as having a reputation as a soldier, an author, a courtier, an explorer, a statesman, and a lover. In some respects he was the Theodore Roosevelt of his age. Doubtless he inherited his genius for gardening from his first parent, Adam. He brought the seed of the cherry from the Azores, and planted the first cherry tree in this famous garden, as it is said all the cherries in the United Kingdom can trace their descent back to Youghal.

We were now only thirty miles from Cork. As we left Youghal, and the landing place of the potato in Ireland, the heavy clouds suddenly made up their minds to decamp. They at once scattered in all directions, and in fifteen minutes the sun was shining just as though it had been with us all morning. Then it was that it occurred to us that the sudden changes of Irish weather were not always a disadvantage. If it rains easy, it also clears away easy.

I was glad to see the fields of Cork again. We followed the railroad line most of the way from Youghal to Cork. We met a train again on this road, and had another noisy greeting from the engine and passenger coaches.

As we neared Cork, and saw the magnificent Cork Harbor, stretching down to Queenstown, I turned to Mike and said:

"Mike, Ireland is a great country, and you and I have seen it the last few days as nobody has ever seen it before. The aeroplane will give to Ireland a new fame throughout the world."

"We have had a big time," said Mike simply, but I knew he was the happiest man on earth, or rather in the air.

As we were circling around preparatory to making a landing, I repeated enthusiastically the words of an Irish poet:

"O Ireland, isn't it grand you look:

Like a bride in her rich adornin'

And with all the pent-up love of my heart,

I bid you the top o' the mornin'."

We landed at 10:00 o'clock on the very field we had left only a few days before.

If Columbus, when he set foot on America, felt any bigger than we did as we stepped out of our aeroplane at Cork that day, he must have felt bigger than Goliath.

CHAPTER XIX

OUR LAST DAY IN IRELAND SEEING TIPPERARY

WE spent the rest of that day around Cork. Going to the steamship office we found our liner would call at Queenstown on the second day. We had one more day for sightseeing.

"Mike," said I, "let us start early tomorrow morning, and spend our last day seeing Tipperary."

"Agreed," said he.

He carefully overhauled the motor, and we had all in readiness for a second flight from Cork the next morning.

We flew direct toward County Tipperary. Our first place of interest was Cashel, the former Capital of Munster.

As we entered Tipperary and skimmed over its green acres, I entertained Mike by quoting to him a description of a Tipperary man:

"Strong is his form, his heart is warm,

His spirit light as any fairy:

His wrath as fearful as the storms

That sweep the hills of Tipperary.

Lead him to fight for Fatherland,

His is no courage cold or wary;

The troops live not on earth could stand

The headlong charge of Tipperary.

But meet him in his cabin rude,

Or walking with his dark-haired Mary,

You'd swear they knew no other mood,

But mirth and love in Tipperary."

When I had finished, Mike returned me the favor by singing, with the motor as an accompaniment, a famous Tipperary song. The words of it are:

"Oh, Paddy, dear, and did you hear the news that's going round?

The shamrock is by law forbid to grow on Irish ground;

No more St. Patrick's Day we'll keep, his color can't be seen,

For there's a bloody law agin the wearin' o' the green.

I met with Napper Tandy, and he tuk me by the hand,

And he said, 'And how's ould Ireland and how does she stand?'

She's the most distressful country that ever yet was seen,

For they're hangin' men and women for the wearin' o' the green."

When he had finished I said:

"Mike, an Irishman could not sing that any better than you."

"An Irishwoman could, though," said Mike, and then he continued, "You ought to have heard Edith sing that very song as we were flying over Dublin. I thought I was in heaven, and was hearing the angels sing."

"When you landed after that trip you both looked as though you had been in the seventh heaven," I answered.

Just then we sighted the rock of Cashel, and our thoughts were turned into other channels. Cashel, like Tara, is only a memory. Formerly it was a place of the greatest importance all over the south of Ireland. Now it is an unimportant village. The famous rock of Cashel still stands, crowned with the ruins of the old Cathedral, King Cormac's Chapel, and a Round Tower. This celebrated rock is a mass of limestone, rising steeply out of the plain to the height of 300 feet. Here formerly the Kings of Munster were crowned, and here, in 1172, Henry II. was declared King of Ireland. St. Patrick preached at Cashel when it was a Royal Court.

We circled the Rock twice to the utter amazement of the inhabitants of the village. I doubt if we made more stir anywhere than in Cashel.

Passing on towards Thurles, we saw one of the finest monastic ruins in Ireland, Holy Cross Abbey. The ruins are of great antiquity, but are well preserved, and they are quite extensive. The Cruciform church is still extant enough to show lines of great beauty. This was a former Sanctuary of the O'Briens of Limerick.

From Thurles we went directly west to Limerick.

Limerick is one of Ireland's oldest cities, and it looks it. It is built on the Shannon river, and Limerick Castle still frowns over that noble stream. This old castle is well preserved.

Limerick, like so many of the towns around the coast of Ireland, was founded by the Danes. It has been the scene of some stirring Irish history. Two famous sieges were endured by this city in the 17th century.

In 1651, the English besieged and captured Limerick under General Ireton. On capturing the city, Ireton hung Bishop O'Brien, an outrage deeply resented by the Irish people.

In 1690 the forces of William II. invested Limerick, after the victory at the Boyne, and the garrison was compelled to capitulate. The treaty of capitulation was signed on a large stone, since called the "Treaty Stone."

This Treaty afterwards was shamefully violated by the English Government, and to this day Limerick is known in Ireland as "The City of the Violated Treaty." As we flew over the city I saw this famous stone, on a pedestal, near Thomond Bridge. I also saw the ancient Cathedral which adorns the city. The present population of Limerick is only 40,000 as the city has lost heavily in recent years by emigration to America. The chief business at present is butter-making, but lace and linen are also produced. There are fine docks and a good export business, as the Shannon is easily navigable at Limerick.

There was one other spot in Ireland we wished to see. We could not finish up our aeroplane trip without flying over Glengariff, which has been called the loveliest spot in all Europe. We made a rapid return flight from Limerick to County Cork. We sped past the Kerry Mountains, beyond which lay Killarney, but we did not attempt to cross them. It was still early in the forenoon when we reached Bantry Bay.

Glengariff means "Rugged Glen" and the scenery is rugged enough in places but it is undoubtedly one of the finest scenes in the world. A mountain stream runs through the lovely valley, which is crossed by many picturesque bridges, before it empties itself into the waters of Bantry Bay. Thackery said if Glengariff were in England, it would be one of the world's wonders. The climate is remarkably mild all the year and the wild flowers grow in profusion. We passed directly over the little village of Glengariff, and saw Cromwell's Bridge. This is a bridge said to have been damaged, as so much else was during Cromwell's visit in the neighborhood.

Our minds, our hearts, our souls were full of the beautiful scenes of the Emerald Isle, when we turned towards Cork for our final flight.

Before we reached the more level land, beyond the hills of Bantry Bay, we had one of our worst experiences with the aeroplane. While crossing a very broken, and hilly stretch of country, covered with stone fences, small cabins, and mountain garden patches, without any warning, the motor again stopped suddenly.

"BEGORRA, IT'S A FOINE BURD."

"BEGORRA, IT'S A FOINE BURD."

I cried out to Mike to land at once. He was compelled to alight, for, when the motor is dead, an aeroplane is like a bird with two broken wings. With the rocky ground, stone fences, and little garden-patches, it was the most difficult descent Mike had to make. He saved the aeroplane from a smash-up only by lighting squarely on the roof of one of the little thatched cabins. As we landed on it, a man, his wife and several children rushed out and gazed at us in silent wonder. We climbed down as best we could, and explained our plight. While the man went away to get some of his neighbors to assist us in getting the aeroplane down on the ground, I looked the cabin over. It was not a beautiful sight when seen close at hand. A vile-smelling manure pile was heaped in front of the door, and the rude stone walls were most unsightly. The thatch looked as ancient as some of the old ruins we had lately seen. The cabin had only one room. Chickens ran in and out along with the children, and as I entered inside, I saw "the pig in the parlor," for the one room was the kitchen, dining room, parlor and bed-room combined. Part of the cooking was done outside during fair weather, and a pot of potatoes were boiling over a peat fire beside the cottage. There was a baby in the mother's arms, and I counted six other children around her. Pallets of straw showed where the nightly rest was obtained. The floor was nothing but hard mother earth. A table, two rough chairs, and a stool, with a rough cupboard completed the furnishings. A few pots lay near the peat fire under the hole, which was meant for a chimney. There was no window. The one door furnished all the light and air.

I found out afterwards that such cabins were occupied only by a comparatively few, even of the poor in Ireland. The Government is at present working among these poor peasants, and in a few years it is expected such hovels will be banished forever from the island. This was a "bog-trotter" cabin, such as is only found in the hilly and desolate regions, where birds, to say nothing of men, find it hard to get a living.

The woman was cordial and self-possessed, and did not seem to mind the squalid surroundings. She offered us some of the cooked potatoes, and as we ate them outside the cabin, taking them in our hands, they tasted as good as though they had been cooked in a palace.

A few neighbors soon gathered and helped us get the aeroplane down from the low roof.

While Mike was getting ready to start again, I talked with the owner of the cabin. He seemed cheerful and pointed out to me his potato patch, his "food and drink."

He told me about the mountains that could be seen from his cabin, and named several of the more important hills. I noticed that a number of the names had the "devil" in them. One peak he called the "devil's Needle." Another hill, with a hollow place in its side was the "devil's Bit." I thought I would see if there was any Irish in him, and I said:

"His Satanic Majesty seems to own a great deal of property among these hills, judging by their names."

"Indade he does, sor," said this son of Erin, "but he is like most of our landlords, he makes his headquarters in London, sor."

I saw it was no difference where you find him, in palace, mansion, villa, cottage, cabin or even hovel, an Irishman is always the same. Everywhere you will find him genial, witty, good-natured. It must be the effect of the Irish atmosphere.

When Mike had the motor going again we soon made our ascent aloft, leaving our Irish cabiners watching us in awe.

We reached Cork again shortly after noon. After a brief rest, we spent the rest of the day in taking the airship to pieces, and re-packing it.

Next morning we were ready for our ocean voyage and took the early train from Cork to Queenstown. Five days later we reached New York. We had been absent considerably less than a month.

Mike has since returned to Ireland. He did not take the aeroplane, but he took along a big trunk. When he returns, as he will in a few weeks, the Connor house in New York State, will have a beautiful young Irish girl as its queen, and my good friend, Mr. O'Neill will come out to America next year to see his daughter, Mrs. Michael Connor. Such was the strange ending of our aeroplane trip. As I think of it, I often say to myself: "It was the result of the Irish atmosphere."

Milton Keynes UK
Ingram Content Group UK Ltd.
UKHW030912151124
451262UK00006B/816